THE HANDBELL CHOIR

"THE BELLS ARE RINGING"

A typical picture and caption used in public relations work.

THE HANDBELL CHOIR

A Manual for
Church, School and Community Groups

By

DORIS WATSON

B.S., M.A., Ed.D.

NEW YORK: THE H. W. GRAY CO., Inc.

Agents for NOVELLO & CO., LTD.
© Copyright 1959 by The H. W. Gray Co., Inc.
International Copyright Secured.

FOREWORD

IN PROVIDING THIS HANDBOOK on the use of handbells for youth choirs in church music, Doris Watson has done the Christian Church a very great service.

One summer during the Second World War a family with handbells visited Keene Valley in the Adirondacks in New York State. Members of the summer community were invited to join in bell ringing. The bells proved an immediate success. As I listened to them it occurred to me that bell ringing would provide a great opportunity for youth in our churches. I immediately ordered a set of bells for The Brick Church in New York City. However, because of war-time conditions we were not able to secure the bells until the spring of 1947. When they arrived they were turned over to our Youth Choir Director who immediately began a training program.

Doris Watson was the Director of the Youth Choir and the Bell Ringers of The Brick Church from 1951 through 1955, and served with great distinction in this capacity. With her background of training in voice, piano, and organ, and her many years in choir work, she brought the art of bell ringing and the contribution of the Bell Choir to a high state of perfection. Out of her experience and success she has written this manual and numerous compositions for handbell ringing. In the companion books of handbell music there are very simple arrangements for beginners and there are more intricate and interesting arrangements for the more skilled and better disciplined groups.

Here in The Brick Church, thanks to Doris Watson and those who preceded her, we have found the Bell Choir a great asset. I recommend the program most highly. It enables youth not merely to discuss religion, but actually to serve in the Church and enter into its worship and ministry.

PAUL AUSTIN WOLFE
Minister
The Brick Presbyterian Church
New York, New York

3

31320

PREFACE

THE PRIMARY DIFFERENCE between a *ringing band* and a *hand-bell choir* lies in the type of music each group rings and the fact that the handbell choir is always identified with the Church wherever it appears. Aside from this, the problems encountered by both ensembles are basically similar whether in the school, in the community or in the Church.

This manual is intended specifically for those interested in knowing more about developing handbell choirs in the Church. However, all of the suggestions are adaptable for use in school and community programs.

ACKNOWLEDGMENTS

This manual would not have been made possible without the cooperation of Mrs. Thomas Kehoe and Mrs. William Kirkley, who typed the manuscript; Miss Margaret Loeffler, who aided in some of the illustrations; The Reverend Stanley Niebruegge, who took some of the photographs; Miss Sharron Hall, whose outstanding work as an assistant director demonstrated the potential ability of young people to accept leadership responsibility; The Reverend Millard G. Roberts, whose public relations work, especially with the press, introduced church handbell ringing to the public; The Reverend George Litch Knight, who provided material through his promotion of the use of handbells in church and hymn festivals; Dr. Paul Austin Wolfe, who introduced handbells to the Church and provided the Foreword; Dr. and Mrs. Clarence Dickinson, who edited the manuscript and provided a constant inspiration to the writer; and The Reverend George M. Watson, the author's husband, who proof-read and advised throughout the writing.

Mention should also be made of the work of Leslie Bidwell, Jack Fisler, Tom Perkins, Arthur Austin and Bob Cahn, who through radio, recording, television and films have promoted handbell choirs, thus helping to create a need for this manual.

The author is also grateful to the young people of The Brick Church Bell Ringers of New York City, The West Side Presbyterian Handbell Choirs of Ridgewood, New Jersey, and The First Presbyterian Church Bell Ringers of Staten Island, New York, for their faithfulness and perseverance in helping develop the various handbell rings and practical suggestions made throughout this manual.

In addition, much valuable material was gained in exchanging ideas with other members of The American Guild of English Handbell Ringers.

DORIS WATSON
Staten Island, New York
January 1959

TABLE OF CONTENTS

TABLE OF CONTENTS

7

TABLE OF CONTENTS

TABLE OF CONTENTS

9

TABLE OF CONTENTS

ILLUSTRATIONS

Body type set in Linotype Bodoni Book and heads in Bodoni Bold — printed letterpress by Herbert-Spencer Inc., New York.

CHAPTER ONE

General Considerations

I. *The Role of the Handbell Choir*

The director, together with the minister and the music committee of the church, will want to decide early the purpose of the handbell choir as well as some general policies regarding its uses. Primarily, the singing choirs of the church are used to glorify God in services of worship. The handbell choir should be just such a worship aid, and should fit naturally into the pattern of the service. Some churches find that some small touch of handbells in each service is appropriate, such as the ringing of *Cambridge Quarters* at the beginning of the service; while others use handbells primarily for special occasions. These decisions concerning the use of the handbell choir in worship are more easily made as the choir grows and can take on varying responsibilities in the service.

The more difficult decisions come in deciding when to use the handbell choir outside the service of worship. There are many demands placed on the choir within the church program, such as ringing for special congregational and organizational functions. These appearances of the bell choir should be limited in order to keep the focus and impact of the choir on the service of worship. Also, other churches and community organizations will make demands on the choir. Although it is not easy to formulate a clear-cut policy, it is wise to establish some guides which will help the director in coping with all these demands.

Many churches have found the answer through reserving the handbell choir almost exclusively for the service of worship, with exceptions being made primarily for charitable institutions or radio and television where it is possible to bring the music of the Church to a wider audience than would be reached in a community gathering.

When a handbell choir needs to be transported, it is good to establish the policy that the church or group sponsoring the appearance provide the transportation and absorb any other necessary expenses. Also for special appearances, the director together with the minister or governing body of the church may want to establish a minimum suggested honorarium. This sum of money can help toward the expense of maintaining the group as well as provide a scholarship fund to help ringers attend handbell festivals and conferences.

There will be some instances when the suggestion of an honorarium would be out of keeping with the spirit of the handbell choir. The ringers would consider as part of their regular activities ringing for festival programs and benevolent organizations such as hospitals and homes for the aged. Also, in considering accepting a ringing engagement for a service of worship, the ability of a church to pay an honorarium should never be the determining factor in whether or not the handbell choir accepts the assignment.

In working with school-age choirs it is important that the director limit ringing engagements so that they do not fall during the school day or on school nights. Occasionally an engagement seems as though it would be such a valuable experience that all the parents may agree with the director's decision to make an exception to this rule.

Although there is a peculiar zest in participating in and listening to handbell ringing, the purpose of the choir cannot be primarily to teach music or to enjoy the ringing itself. Actu-

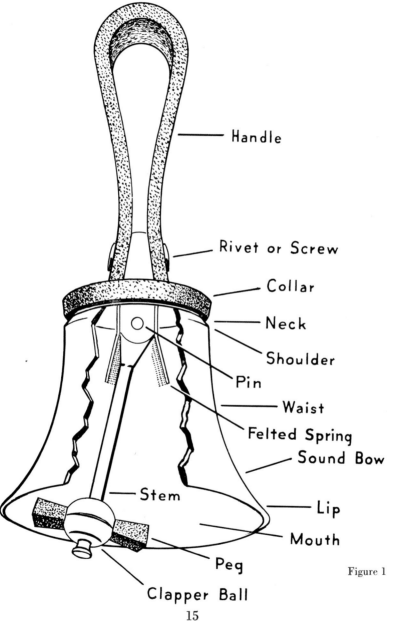

Handle

Rivet or Screw

Collar

Neck

Shoulder

Pin

Waist

Felted Spring

Sound Bow

Stem

Lip

Mouth

Peg

Clapper Ball

Figure 1

ally there is a two-fold Christian educational purpose for the very existence of the choir. First, the ringer learns something about discipline in that each one has a specific job which must be done if the group is to survive. Second, the ringers discover that many times they are in the position of bringing the Church and its message to assortments of people with varying religious beliefs. Through their ringing and general attitude toward their choir they are often able to make the Christian faith and its characteristic joy contagious.*

II. *Range*

The suggested set of handbells referred to throughout this manual ranges from the G above middle C on the piano to two octaves above that, with all of the chromatic tones between. In ordering English handbells, this is the two-octave set beginning with 18 G (the G above middle C) and going through 4 G (the highest G in the twenty-five bell set).** All foundries do not utilize the same system for numbering their handbells. An example of this is the Dutch foundry, Petit and Fritsen, which numbers each bell separately beginning with the *lower* bells and numbering *upward* through the higher bells. Numbers 20 through 44 would be comparable to 18 G through 4 G on the English Whitechapel bells. (In ordering Dutch handbells it is

---

* "If God wills it, we hope to form a Bell Choir for the purpose of spreading His message as you have done and are doing."

"The spirit of cooperation that enlightened the features of your young people was an inspiration."

"Please tell your young players that we here in Minneapolis were inspired by their playing."

— *Excerpts from correspondence received by the writer.*

** Some handbell choir directors prefer the two chromatic octaves beginning with 19 F through 5 F. Considering a variety of church music and keys, either set is equally adaptable for church ringing. The writer prefers the G to G set as on the whole it provides a little more brilliance, a quality desirable in handbell ringing.

important to keep in mind that the C pitched an octave *above* middle C is called, in their literature, "Middle C.")

The purchaser should either order the bells by designating the pitches desired, or write the foundry of his choice for complete details. Some customers may find it easier to deal with handbell distributors in their area.

The addition of a large bell or two adds interest and further color to a choir's ringing. It is suggested that when possible the church purchase the G bell just below middle C, or in ordering English handbells, 25 G. This bell can be incorporated at the beginning or ending of many numbers rung in the key of G.

Two chromatic octaves provide a minimum number of tones for achieving variety and color in ringing. The bell music published in conjunction with this manual embraces this range.

When supplementing this basic set many fine effects can be developed through the further addition of lower and higher bells. The F and F# above middle C are particularly valuable. The lowest handbell, the C below middle C (29 C, in ordering English handbells), although it is quite heavy to hold and can be used only sparingly, produces a tone which is a decided asset in numbers written in the keys of C and F. This bell, however, can best be used in progressions with the G and/or F below middle C (25 G and/or 26 F, in ordering English bells).

Some choirs have had considerable success with the higher bells from the highest G up through the C three octaves above middle C (1 C, in ordering English bells). The foundry will also make higher bells upon request. In ordering extra higher bells it is usually best to get a minimum of the next two higher bells as a starter; namely, 4 G# and 3 A. G# alone would not be valuable, but by adding A the basic coverage would be pro-vided for an additional key.

17

III. *Notation of Handbell Music*

Throughout this manual and the music, the notation for the handbells is one octave lower than the actual pitch of the bells. This is done for convenience in notating on the treble

staff, the range as it appears being:  but

actually sounding:

A set of handbells pitched one octave lower than the suggested set would be quite heavy to manage easily and too resonant for the majority of handbell arrangements, and therefore is not recommended.

There are various systems of notation which can be employed, but the use of basic music notation confined to the treble clef is highly recommended. Regular notation provides continuity between handbell music and conventional music. The exception to this is when notating the lowest or the highest bells. Rather than adding a confusing and space-consuming number of leger lines the tones can be noted through the use of an alphabet letter. Thus, the actual tone of G below middle C,

when used in a chord, would be notated:

The actual sound of this chord would be:

If a choir owns and uses many low bells it might be advisable to use music written in both the treble and bass clefs. However, since low bells are especially resonant and therefore are used sparingly when rung with the smaller high-pitched bells, most of the basic notation can be done on the treble staff.

IV. *Pitch of the Organ*

It is wise to know before ordering the handbells whether or not the organ of the church is standard in pitch. Because each bell is tuned separately by hand, and tested by ear and electronically, it would be a rather easy matter to suggest the pitch needed by a particular church, if this pitch varies from the standard. However, it would not be possible for bells tuned to other than standard pitch to ring with the majority of bell choirs at festivals.

When a choir participates in a service of worship at another church, it is necessary to check on the pitch of the organ if the handbells are to be used as an integral part of the service.

V. *Status of Procuring Bells*

Most of the handbells presently used in church work in this country are English in origin, coming primarily from the Whitechapel Foundry in London.* The tone of these bells is ideally suited for work in the church.

Now, enterprising companies in the Netherlands are working toward the end of having handbells stocked in this country and founding them here.**

---

* Whitechapel Bell Foundry, 32 and 34 Whitechapel Road, London, E.1, England.
** The company most active at this time in a campaign to conquer the problems of production and marketing is the Petit & Fritsen Bell Founders of Aarle-Rixtel, Holland. (U.S. office: Fritsen Brothers, 605 Waukegan Road, Deerfield, Illinois.)

19

VI. *Overtones*

A handbell, unlike a tower bell, is tuned to just one prominent overtone. This overtone is the twelfth above the strike tone and has proved to be especially suitable for handbell arrangements. The fact that there is but one discernable overtone makes a great variety of chord progressions possible with a minimum of dissonance.

The bells of any particular foundry should be tested for accuracy of the strike tone as well as the overtone.* If there is a variation in the overtone of each handbell within a set, the customer will have to decide whether or not the overall tone of the handbells is pleasant or unpleasant to him. Some directors have not found this variation in overtones a problem.

If the overtone of a handbell is too loud in relation to its strike tone, there is a tendency for the strike tone to be obscured. When this is the general characteristic of a set of bells the harmonies of a handbell arrangement are not as clearly defined, and in a full arrangement the overtones can become overpowering, virtually obliterating the melody.

Before purchasing bells, the potential buyer would do well to consult a handbell choir director or a member of the American Guild of English Handbell Ringers for advice. The Guild is a national organization which, through annual national meetings and regional meetings, keeps abreast of recent trends in handbells.

---

* The Whitechapel handbell has an almost completely accurate overtone.

CHAPTER TWO

The Care of the Handbell

I. *Housing for Handbells*

One of the first things a director will want to consider when his bells arrive is an adequate place to house them when not in use, bearing in mind the fact that there will be occasions when the handbells must be transported. Various solutions to this problem have been devised.

1. *Partitioned boxes*: The first, and perhaps the most adaptable case, takes the form of a box with a hinged lid on the top. This box is deep enough to accommodate the largest bell from clapper to handle in an erect position. The box is subdivided into a compartment for each bell. At the bottom of each of these compartments is placed a 1½ inch thick piece of plywood with a hole drilled wide enough to allow the clapper to swing freely while the lip of the bell rests on the plywood. Foam rubber used at the base of each compartment can be substituted for the drilled plywood.

The overall size of the cabinet will depend on the number of handbells in the set. Usually between eleven and fifteen bells can be stored in each cabinet. To determine the number and size of cabinets needed, place paper on the floor and arrange the bells on the paper using the space most economically. Leave enough space between each bell to allow for the thickness of the plywood used in making the compartments. Keeping in mind that each cabinet must not be too big for carrying, outline the bells on the paper, remove bells and outline compartment squares with a double line comparable to the thickness of the plywood, and thus complete the pattern.

For the suggested twenty-five bell set, plus one large bell, two cabinets will be necessary. See Figure 2, below, for an

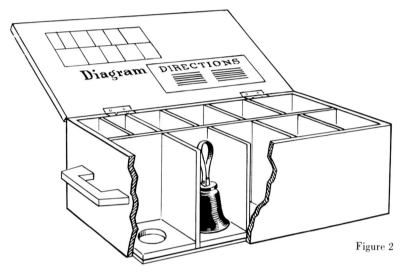

Figure 2

interior sketch of this type cabinet. There should be a diagram on the lid designating where each bell is to be placed, and also some general instructions for preserving the luster of the hand-bells. If gloves are used in ringing (see Section III of this chapter) there should be a place in the cabinet to store them. Clips on the inside of the lid would be one way to hold the gloves and by labeling the clips, each person would be assured of having his own gloves. Otherwise, they could be simply dropped into the compartments with the bells.

These cabinets are best made out of seven-ply and three-ply plywood. The seven-ply is used for the box itself and the one main division across the center. The three-ply is used for the smaller compartments.

The compartments can either come a little over half way up to the top of the box, or they can come up even to the top. The advantages of the former are that the handbell handles are a little more accessible and the cabinets are somewhat lighter. The main advantage of the latter type is that in transporting the bells they have a little more protection.

On each end of the cabinet place a metal carrying handle. Try to find a large comfortable handle as the cases are difficult to manage on long hauls. Padlocks can easily be affixed to the lid.

This type of cabinet is best suited for the transporting of handbells since the cabinet easily fits into the trunk of a car and the bells rest securely in the compartments. While casters can be mounted on this type of cabinet, they tend to make it less adaptable in storing where space is a consideration, as one cannot be placed atop the other.

2. *Tiered cabinets*: Another type of cabinet consists of two rows of wooden pegs from which the bells are suspended in chromatic order. There is a pair of hinged doors on one side for easy accessibility and the cabinet rests on casters. A handle is affixed to the top frame. Two cabinets are necessary for the suggested twenty-five bell set.

The chief advantage of this type of cabinet lies in the fact that it rolls easily from closet into rehearsal room. However, it is awkward to carry and to use in transit. The casters are of no advantage in surmounting stairs. Owners of such cabinets usually transport their bells in plain or specially designed boxes, protecting the bells with flannel bags.

If it is not anticipated that the bells will be transported often, these cabinets have a further advantage of good looks since they can be fashioned into attractive pieces of workmanship. See Figure 3, below.

Figure 3

Some directors who use these cabinets have an extra piece of wood hinged to each shelf or used separately. Each piece is about 4 inches wide, an inch deep and the length of the shelf. It is flat on one side and cut to fit the shape of the lips of the bells on the other. This shaped side can be lined with a narrow strip of felt or rubber insulation.* To release the bells it folds outward, and when the bells are put away, it folds in and around the lips of the bells. See Figure 4, page 25.

3. *Manufactured cases*: One type of cabinet for handbells has been manufactured by Petit and Fritsen. Providing these

---

* "Flan" (a self-adherent flannel) or "Stik-Rite" (sponge rubber weather stripping which comes in various narrow widths) can be purchased at most hardware stores.

cabinets fit an owner's particular set of bells, it is a convenient way of transporting them. See Figure 5, page 29.

4. *Unpartitioned boxes*: Bells wrapped in flannel bags can also be stored and transported in a strong box with a lid and handles and no partitions. When this is done the bells are

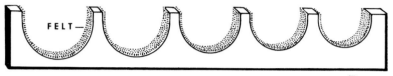

FELT

Figure 4

placed on their sides with the heavier bells at the bottom of the box and the lighter bells on top.

5. *Partitioned footlockers*: If special boxes are not constructed it is usually possible to find adequately sized footlockers. These should have compartments of various sizes built into them. Each compartment should be lined with a thick-napped material such as velour; and foam rubber can be used at the base of the compartments. This provides adequate protection for storage and transportation.

6. *Storage racks*: Some directors use pegs built into a stationary cabinet or closet which can be locked. Thus the bells hang in the practice room with the advantage of easy accessibility. For transportation, boxes and flannel bags must be used.

II. *The Use of Flannel Bags*

In addition to the use of cabinets, the bells should be further protected in storing by being covered with flannel bags.*

These bags protect the bright luster of the bells, cushion them

---

* "Pacific Cloth" (a specially treated flannel which is sold by the yard) is recommended because it prevents tarnishing, and contains no substance detrimental to the metal when used in rubbing the bell.

against damage, and somewhat protect the inner mechanism of the bells against moisture hazards in a damp climate. (See Section IV of this chapter, which deals with the problems of dampness and oiling.) They should be used at all times, in storage as well as in transit. Each bag should be marked with the bell letter for identification to insure proper fit. The open end of the bag can be fitted with a drawstring or a ribbon can be attached to the outside of the bag. These bags cover the bells leaving the handles exposed.

III. *Polishing*

A handbell should never be polished to a high luster with a commercial polish. Tests have indicated that *there is no polish which does not remove some small amount of metal.** Used continuously on a handbell, this would eventually affect its pitch and tonal quality.**

The most effective and safest method of preserving the luster of the bell is either to wear gloves at all times when handling the bell and/or to rub the surface, inside and out, with a flannel or other soft dry cloth. The bell bags themselves can be used when necessary. This rubbing should be done, if possible, at the close of each rehearsal or performance. Each ringer should be responsible for his assigned handbells, rubbing them and enclosing them in the flannel bags before storing them in

---

* While most commercial polishes are abrasive, a certain few such as Noxon work on an acid principle. This latter type should be safer if the director is willing to sacrifice the accurate pitch of a handbell for high luster. Some directors use it to polish a few bells at the close of each rehearsal, covering the complete set in a period of some three or four months.

** The writer has had the experience of having two choirs ring together one year, and finding that the following year when the same music was attempted by the same two choirs it was impossible for them to ring together. One of the choirs had consistently used polish on its handbells with the result that the pitch of the handbells was altered sufficiently so that the two choirs could not ring together.

the cabinet. Ringers not using gloves should further be instructed never to place their fingers on the bell metal. When using special ringing effects demanding the use of the fingers on the handbell, the ringer must wear gloves. (For an illustration of this see the description of the dampened ring, Chapter Three, Section II, 14.) Finger contact can damage the surface of the bell and eventually will effect the tone of the bell.

After considerable use the handbells may become dull and dark in color. A mild discoloration will not alter the pitch but may tend to mellow the bell tone. However, when bells have excessive contact with fingers and/or are not adequately rubbed after each use, a dark film accumulates. This can be equally as damaging as the promiscuous use of polish. When this dark film does gather it is necessary to remove most of it by buffing or polishing. *Do not attempt to restore the original luster of the bell.*

IV. *Oiling*

When handbells have been in use for some time, a clicking sound often develops at the base of the clapper.* To remedy this a drop of sewing machine or bicycle oil should be placed on each side of the stem of the clapper where it is fitted to the staple-pin on which it swings. This should be done only when needed. An all-purpose oil is definitely not recommended. Instead, a good grade sewing machine oil purchased from a sewing machine shop or an exclusive bicycle oil procurable at a bicycle shop should be kept available for use on the handbells.

Occasionally in very damp climates the clappers will stick and not bounce back to starting position. When this happens,

---

* For this and subsequent references to the parts of a handbell, see Figure 1, page 15.

the bells should be put near some gentle, drying heat until the dampness is gone. If clicking develops when the bounce of the clapper is restored, the treatment prescribed above should be employed. Do not apply oil if the dampness is still in the bell.

V. *Care of the Leather*

1. *Clappers*: Sometimes a leather peg on the clapper ball becomes loose. It can be tightened by removing the leather from the clapper and pressing or trimming down the end removed. This treatment furnishes a wider base when the peg is reinserted and it is then usually tight enough to prevent twisting. The trimming of the ends also prevents them from meeting inside the clapper ball. When screw lines are discernable in the two side holes on the clapper ball the leather pegs should be reinserted by a twisting or screwing-in motion.

The leather peg can also become too dry. To prevent this it is good to apply, every three months or when the leather looks dry and about to crack, a good combination of neatsfoot oil (about 60%) and lanolin (40%).

2. *Handles*: Usually when bells are used fairly constantly the oil from the hands keeps the handles lubricated quite adequately. However, at least once a year the leather on the handles should be rubbed with oil. When gloves are used in ringing, the handles should be lubricated three or four times a year. The solution suggested for the leather on the clapper pegs is recommended, and a small bottle should be kept available for use on the leather parts of the handbells.

VI. *Overall Reconditioning*

When a set of handbells has been used over a long period of time, various conditions arise which can be disturbing to the ringers. Clappers can become too loose, leather on clappers can become too worn, handles can become limp and occasionally the tone of a bell can become impaired. Even new bells have varying characteristics to which ringers must become accustomed. However, when these characteristics become detrimental to the performance of a handbell choir, the bells should be reconditioned. This can usually be done by making arrangements with the foundry where the bells were purchased to have them returned and attended to. Two or three months must be allowed for this procedure, and the arrangements must be made well in advance.

A bell which has been dropped and cracked or is otherwise unusable must be reordered immediately. Such a bell cannot be repaired, although the metal can be used in re-casting.

Several members of the American Guild of English Handbell Ringers have been experimenting in the realm of minor repairs. As time goes on it should be possible to receive help by contacting this organization.

Figure 5

CHAPTER THREE

Learning to Ring

I. *General Information on Holding the Handbell*

Through the centuries ringers have held and rung handbells in many different fashions. These were acceptable and achieved a purpose. However, for the sake of the visual uniformity and the precision ringing which is essential to the church handbell choir, bells should be rung predominantly in one way.

The handle should be grasped, fingers encircling it, close to the neck of the bell. For greater control of specific rings, some ringers place their thumb on the flat part of the handle facing them. Again, this must be done on the portion of the handle closest to the neck of the bell. Some gain even further control by placing the thumb against the collar of leather which surrounds the neck of the bell. This is especially good for a quick, sharp ring.

The starting position of the handbell for most rings is mouth upward, with a slight backward tilt so that the clapper falls back toward the ringer rather than forward. Holding the bell fairly close to his shoulder, the ringer moves the bell forward in a downward arc, culminating the ring with a quick downward flick of the wrist so that the clapper contacts the bell. The bell is brought back to starting position in an upward arc. The complete movement is a horizontal oval, with the strike occurring at the point farthest away from the ringer. At the strike point the elbow is crooked at approximately a ninety degree angle and the bell is in a nearly horizontal position. This strike point will be referred to throughout the description of rings as the ring position.

At the end of the execution of most rings the bell should be in a nearly vertical position. Care should be taken to keep the backward tilt (essential for getting the clapper in starting position) minimal. If a ringer tilts the mouth of a bell too far back at the conclusion of a ring some of the tone is lost.

II. *Various Rings and Their Symbols*

1. *Straight Ring*: This ring, described in the preceding paragraph, is the ring most often used. It can be controlled to produce a soft, medium, or loud tone. The speed and size of the arc as well as the force of the strike are important in determining the tone. For uniformity in ringing and a variety of rings, the director will want to experiment with these three variable components of the straight ring. When the straight ring is used in a melodic line, it is obviously louder than when used as accompaniment. At no time should a bell be rung so stridently that the tone is distorted, but rather each ringer should find in his bell a way to produce a rich, round, pleasing tone. Occasionally a handbell will produce a better tone if the leather clapper peg strikes the bell near either end of the peg rather than directly in the center. There is no symbol for the straight ring. An example of a number using all straight rings is the short response "Softly Now the Light of Day."*

2. *Back Ring*: In executing the back ring the bell is held at ring position. Some ringers may need to hold the bell in a completely horizontal position in order to gain momentum for the complete ring. With a flick of the wrist backward, the bell

---

* All examples are taken from the *Book of Handbell Music, Set I*, published by H. W. Gray Co., Inc., N. Y.

is rung, and at the completion of this ring the bell is in the starting position of the straight ring. Actually the ringer must guard against bringing the bell too far back lest the tone be lost. To keep the bell in a nearly vertical position the thumb should act as a guard by being placed against the collar or flat part of the handle. This ring usually produces a softer tone and is used for special effects. However, the two notes can be rung with equal force if necessary. In music notation it is indicated by $\searrow$. An example of this ring is found in "Come, Ye Faithful, Raise the Strain." It can also be used for an unaccented boom tone (or grace note) such as is seen in the second version of the hymn tune *Rathbun*.

3. *Accented Ring*: This ring is equivalent to the straight ring, but is executed with a quicker flick of the wrist. It is usually used in emphasizing melodic line. The symbol for the accented ring is $\nearrow$. An example of this ring is found in "Angels We Have Heard on High."

4. *Roll*: Moving the bell from starting to ring position, the wrist is flicked forward and back, causing the clapper to contact the bell on both sides in a quick succession of rings equivalent to the value of the note. Because of the individual difference in handbells it is sometimes necessary to move the lower arm back and forth together with the wrist in order to execute a smooth roll. The symbol for this is $\nearrow$. This ring may be played on one note of a chord to emphasize the melody (such as is found in *Old Hundredth*) or simultaneously on two or more tones as an accompaniment. This latter effect is somewhat similar to the tremolando effect of carillon music,* and is found in "Jacob's Ladder."

---

* "Tremolando: The alternating of two or more notes forming a harmony." *An Introduction to Carillon Technique and Arranging* by Wendell Westcott, Petit and Fritsen.

5. *Semi-Roll*: This is the alternating of two tones, usually a third apart although it can be any interval. This ring must be done by one ringer. It should be a steady motion resulting in an even value for each note. There are two ways of achieving this ring. In using either method the ringer holds the higher bell in the left hand. The preferred method, which usually seems easier for the ringer, is achieved by having the ringer ring a straight ring with the left hand, followed by a back ring with the right hand. Then he must quickly reverse the procedure by ringing a back ring with the left hand and a straight ring with the right hand. The skill comes in keeping the notes equally spaced. Another method is for the ringer to ring a straight ring with the left hand, a straight ring with the right, a back ring with the left hand and a back ring with the right. He continues this motion in equally spaced notes until the complete ring is concluded. The symbol for the semi-roll is ✕ , with the two alternating notes designated in the proper time value; i.e.,

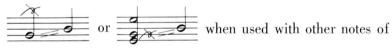 or when used with other notes of

the chord.

A semi-roll can be completely notated as found in the second version of "Angels We Have Heard on High."

6. *Double Semi-Roll*: This ring usually involves the alternating of two tones a whole or a half step apart with two other tones a whole or half step apart. This ring can be performed by using one of the same two methods described for the semi-roll. The difference is that two ringers execute it together. It is

notated  or when used with other

33

notes in the chord. This is especially effective in secular numbers, and is found in "Jingle Bells."

7. *Front Double*: This is a combination of first the straight and then the back ring. Each tone is equivalent to one-half the note value. The symbol for this is ‖ . The accent normally occurs on the first of the two notes, although the ring can be executed with the tones equally accented. This ring is used in the Swiss folk song "O Nightingale, Awake."

8. *Back Double*: This is a combination of first the back and then the straight ring, with each ring being equivalent to half the value of the note. In this ring the second note is usually the accented tone. The symbol for this is N . "O Come, O Come Emmanuel" contains an example of this ring.

9. *Front Double* 3, 5, 7 *and* 9: These rings begin and continue as a front double, ending on the beat. The number indicates the total number of straight and back rings needed to complete the pattern. The value of the note the symbol accompanies determines the speed of the clapper. The symbols for these are $\frac{3}{\|}$, $\frac{5}{\|}$, $\frac{7}{\|}$ and $\frac{9}{\|}$. An example of the front double 3 is found in "Jacob's Ladder."

10. *Back Double* 3: This ring begins with a back ring, then the straight ring, ending with the back ring. It is most often used alternately with the front double 3 in triplet patterns. The symbol for this is $\frac{3}{N}$. This alternating effect used in "Jacob's Ladder."

11. *Boom Tone*: This is an accented ring on a low bell immediately preceding a chord. Its notation is similar to that of a grace note, ♪ . However, it differs from the grace note in being an *accented* tone. The time interval between the boom tone and the chord depends upon the musical context. (See "Ringing Some Changes C-G.")

34

12. *Boom Roll*: This begins with the straight ring and is followed with a slow, soft, steady roll for the complete value of the note. The straight ring can be either accented or unaccented. The boom roll usually accompanies a half, dotted half or whole note. The boom occurs on the downbeat and the roll usually occurs on the second beat and it continues for the complete value of the note. The symbol used is *B⁓*. If the boom is to be accented the symbol would be *⁄B⁓*. This effect is employed in "Love Lives Again."

13. *Dampened Tone*: This is usually a straight ring dampened either by touching a gloved finger to the lip of the bell or by bringing it back until it touches the shoulder. This ring is most often used to clarify certain harmonic structures where the prolonging of a tone would cause too great a harmonic dissonance. It is especially valuable in cadences where many tones can run into the final chord causing a blurring or distortion of sound. This is clearly shown in the final cadence of "Angels We Have Heard on High." To preserve a smooth flow in the ringing of a cadence, all the ringers except those ringing on the final chord should lightly touch the metal just as the final chord is being rung or a few seconds later. *No bell should be dampened before the final chord begins to sound.* The symbol for this is *d-* and it appears above the last chord in the cadence.

There may be instances of key changes or extremely chromatic passages where this device would be valuable. In recording it is good to be critical of an overabundance of dissonant overtones. However, since dampening is artificial to the nature of the bell it should be used sparingly and with discretion.

Some directors use dampening consistently for the final chord of a number after the chord has sounded a reasonable amount of time. The symbol for this is *d* placed above the chord to which it applies. This device is certainly valuable when in a final chord with a large range of tones one or two of the bells resound much longer than the others.

This ring, which can be accented or unaccented, can also be used to create special effects, such as are found in "My Grandfather's Clock."

For a more unusual effect which causes a double sound, the ring is begun with a back ring ending with the bell brought quickly to the shoulder. The symbol is the same with the addition of the sign for a back ring. It can be either accented or unaccented.

14. *Dampened Ring*: This is a straight ring with the bell held in a gloved hand by the waist instead of the handle. This produces a dull-sounding staccato effect which is seldom appropriate for church music. This ring is hard on the mechanism of the handbell, as the ringer must ring very forcibly in order to get a tone. Occasionally it might make an acceptable variation for harpsichord music which is often used in the church handbell choir repertoire. It is also good for novelty numbers such as "Pop Goes the Weasel." It should be used sparingly, if at all. The symbol for this is **D**.

15. *Swing*: Occasionally one or more bells can be swung by beginning with a straight ring, but instead of bringing the handbell back to starting position, the ringer drops his arm to his side and the arm and the bell swing to and fro as the bell continues to speak. During the swinging the mouth of the bell faces downward. To prevent the clapper from striking the bell as the arm swings downward and then back almost to starting position, the wrist is turned to face slightly upward. The symbol for this is **S** accompanied by a number which indicates the number of complete swings plus the strike tone before the bell is brought

back to starting position, *i.e.*, $\frac{3}{8}$. The complete ring should be equivalent in time to the value of the note. "Sweet Hour of Prayer" demonstrates a swing.

16. *Gyro-Ring*: To accomplish this ring the ringer must execute a straight ring; but instead of bringing the hand back to starting position he circles the bell, mouth faced straight forward, in a counter-clockwise motion for a designated number of complete revolutions. The complete arm is involved in the motion, which results in a substantial gyrophonic effect. The symbol for this is ↺ , with a number inside indicating the number of complete revolutions plus the initial strike tone. This complete gyrophonic effect must be equivalent in time to the value of the note. The hymn tune *Aberystwyth* includes the gyro-ring.

17. *Four-Bell Ring*: In this ring each ringer holds four bells, and in covering the tones of the diatonic scale, only two ringers standing side by side are required. The ringer to the left holds in his left hand the highest tone and the third below. In the key of G this would be high G and E. In his right hand he holds F♯ and D. The second ringer holds in his left hand C and A, in his right hand B and G. With the higher of the two handbells designated for each hand held in starting position, the lower bell should be placed so that its handle rests on the handle of the higher bell. With the higher bell in starting position, the mouth of the lower bell points to the right and slightly upward as the handles rest together. See Figure 6, page 38. The clappers of the bells must then be arranged so that each can be struck individually or together. This ring demands patience and experimentation in holding the bells, and is purely a novelty used only when two or more ringers want to spend extra time for a special program. Any diatonic melody confined to an octave makes interesting material for a four-bell

ring executed by two ringers ("Joy to the World," "Blue Bells of Scotland," etc.).

Figure 6

18. *Bell Trill*: Musically this is similar to a regular trill, with the auxiliary note being either above or below the primary

note. On bells it is executed by one ringer. It can occur in a cadence between the seventh and eighth notes of the scale, or it can appear between any two diatonic tones of the scale. In his left hand the ringer holds the higher of the two bells. He rings a straight ring with his left hand, followed quickly by a straight ring with his right hand. Then he goes directly into a back ring with his left hand, following this by rolling both bells. The rolls begin slowly and gradually increase in tempo. When the ring appears in a cadence the ringer concludes it with a back double with the left hand, ending the ring with the next notated tone, which in the cadence would be an accented downbeat. There is no concluding back double when the trill appears in the music other than in the cadence; however, the ring should end on the primary tone of the trill. The skill in executing either type of trill is in keeping the first three rings evenly spaced and then going into the double roll without any perceptible break. The symbol for the cadence trill is *TR* with the primary tone as well as the auxiliary tone noted as follows:

 . The symbol for the regular trill is *tr* with the

two tones involved noted as follows:  . For an

example of the use of the cadence trill see the hymn tune *St. Theodulph.*

19. *Rolled Back Double*: This ring begins with a soft roll, increases in strength of tone and ends with an accented back double. This ring usually occurs on the final chord of a cadence. The symbol is ⟋𝄐 . The same effect can be achieved when two tied notes are connected by a roll, such as appears

in the hymn tune *O Quanta Qualia*. In this instance it is used to emphasize the melodic line.

III. *The Importance of the Position of the Symbols*

A symbol placed above a chord applies to the complete chord. A symbol placed to the right side of a note affects only that one note.

IV. *Dynamics*

Many dynamic shades are possible, and should be employed by the bell choir. It is most imperative to have the melody emphasized, especially in full harmonic passages. When the melody appears in a position in the chord other than at the top this principle becomes invariable.

Some choirs employ the effective technique of vividly ringing a short number, then repeating it softly, or vice versa.

Directors should establish a set of easily recognized signals which will indicate to the ringers the dynamics which should be employed at any given time during performance.

In order to develop good dynamic shading the director should use various exercises at the beginning of each handbell choir session or as needed. (See Chapter Six, which deals with rehearsal techniques.)

CHAPTER FOUR

The Appearance of the Handbell Choir

I. *Regular Formation in Performance*

In considering both the music and the appearance of a handbell choir, the most satisfying formation is to stand in a semi-circle or a horseshoe. With the director facing the choir the bells are arranged scale-wise beginning with the lower bells to the director's left. For the suggested twenty-five bell set between twelve and fifteen ringers are ideal. This would mean that each ringer would be responsible for one, or at the most, two diatonic tones with their accidentals. The diatonic tone and its accidentals will vary according to the key in which the music is written. For example, in the key of A flat major, the D ringer holds the bell marked "C#," but obviously in the key of D major, the C ringer holds the C# bell.*

If only twelve or fewer ringers are used, those on either end of the formation should have the greater number of bells since these are used less frequently in most arrangements. Because the appearance of a bell choir is important, the shorter ringers are placed at either end of the formation, with the taller ringers in the center.

If a choir does intricate chromatic work, or has fewer than eight or ten ringers, it may be necessary to place the handbells on a table.** In this event each ringer covers more than the three or four bells suggested above. Using a table is not desirable

---

* Some handbell sets are coming through stamped with only flats on the handles or with flats imprinted on one side and sharps on the other.

** A few choirs prefer to work this way, but if too few ringers are used the group loses its identity as a choir.

for church handbell ringing since it detracts from the atmosphere of a service of worship, it reduces somewhat the precision of the ringing, and it makes the choir less mobile and adaptable to the physical surroundings.

Another method enabling each ringer to handle an additional handbell is to have a heavy ribbon or cord attached to the handle of each bell. The handbells are hung around the neck, with one bell in either hand and the third hanging mouth downward about waist level. When the ringer finds it necessary to ring his third bell he quickly exchanges one of his bells for the extra bell. This system, which eliminates the necessity for bending over for extra bells, is most useful when the music remains comparatively simple chromatically. However, in music heavy with accidentals, or in a program where several key changes are employed, it is often necessary for some of the bells to be rung by several different ringers.* In choir work where there is rather extensive repertoire, the use of ribbons or cords is usually impractical.

A director might want to have a detachable cord or two available for use in processing or parading.

II. *Practice Formation*

This formation is exactly the same as that used in performance, except that the ringers are seated. Ringers hold only the bells used in a particular number, placing the additional bells at their feet.

---

* Passing a bell from ringer to ringer can be avoided if a director makes permanent bell assignments regardless of the various keys of the music or the number of times a certain bell is rung.

III. *Processing Formation*

In processing or marching, the two ends of the regular formation are drawn together so that each ringer has a partner. The director or a designated leader (preferably the ringer with the highest or lowest bells) should precede the group, especially in parading, so he can turn around and face the ringers to give directions.

IV. *Robes*

When choirs make appearances they should be robed. These robes can be similar to those of the singing choirs of the church, and *should* be if all of the ringers are also members of a singing choir. Having identical robes lessens confusion when both singing and ringing choirs are participating in the same service.

Some ringing choirs which use singers' robes add a distinctive touch to their attire by using either a cross, a stole or some other accessory not used by the singing choir.

If the members of the ringing choir are drawn from several singing choirs, each of which uses a different robe, then it would be better for the ringing choir to use the robes used by the oldest singers who are ringers* or have separate attire to be used for performances.

Some handbell choirs have separate costumes or robes for concert appearances. All kinds of ingenuity can be used in deciding what general pattern to use — whether it be medieval in flavor or starkly contemporary.

---

* This system would eliminate the need to provide the younger ringers with new robes when they become old enough for the older singing choir.

CHAPTER V

The Role of the Director

I. *Teaching*

The director's primary purpose musically is to teach basic principles as well as the art of ringing bells. More importantly, if a handbell choir is going to be effective, the teacher has the job of helping each ringer realize his value to the group. Reliability, self-control and a willingness to sacrifice social engagements when the need arises are disciplines essential to a well-knit group. In the church, the teacher has the further job of helping the ringers understand the challenge they face in communicating through their music and their attitudes the good news of the Christian message wherever they may be.

To be a good bell teacher the director must have a great deal of patience and a personal interest in each of the ringers. He must be enthusiastic about bells. Although a fine sense of musicianship is essential, these other characteristics are even more necessary.

The director should also be able to help the ringers understand the importance of forgetting any ringing errors they happen to make in performance. When a ringer stops to dwell on a mistake, especially when ringing from memory, he is likely to make several others. Not dwelling on errors is good mental discipline. The director should emphasize this.

II. *Developing Leadership*

There are many instances when it is necessary for the director to use a student as director, as is the case when the church organist is also the bell choir director. This assistant or student director should be a person from the bell choir who is familiar with the techniques of the director and who is willing to emulate them.

The choosing of this person should begin at the very first rehearsal of the new handbell choir. At that time the director should give each ringer an opportunity to direct, and it will soon be evident which ringer, or ringers, have the best abilities. Within two or three rehearsals the director will want to choose the one person who seems best qualified and who is willing to devote the extra time to perfecting his directing techniques. Obviously this person should have had some musical training and should be a person who commands the respect of the group.

Some suggested duties of the student director are: to direct when necessary, to assist in caring for the music, to take charge of the robing if there is no choir mother, to substitute for an absent ringer if there is no established system for taking care of absenteeism. (See Section V of this chapter, which deals with the purpose of training a second bell choir.)

The student director together with the director must realize the importance of keeping alive a sense of fun and discovery in rehearsals and performances. It is especially necessary to keep this element in mind when working with beginning groups.

A student director in using methods and repertoire completely familiar to him, perhaps even monotonous for this reason, must in no way disturb the refreshing spirit of discovery that prevails during the rehearsal, especially of the beginning choir, by developing an attitude which clearly says, "This is old stuff." The student director, as well as any good teacher, finds that he can always learn and discover with a group if he

45

approaches his job with a creative mind, regardless of the oldness or newness of the material being presented.

From time to time the director will find it profitable to give other ringers an opportunity to direct, thereby developing talent for future use and for emergencies. Developing such leadership is good for the morale of the group.

One way to give various student directors from the choir opportunity to direct is to have the *Cambridge Quarters*, or some other simple musical pattern, rung at the beginning of each church service. This ringing should follow the organ prelude and precede the processional hymn or call to worship. There should be a rotation of ringers and student directors so that each member of the choir has an equal opportunity to serve.*

The importance of ringing with complete assurance at the beginning of each service must be emphasized, as ringers tend to take an easy assignment lightly and can become careless. Actually, ringing at the beginning of worship sets the tone for the whole service. Since the entire choir would not be involved in ringing each Sunday, the ringers can be divided into two or three groups, and it can be set up so that the same group rings for a month at a time. This system eases the burden of scheduling and provides the opportunity for a group to improve each Sunday.

III. *Meeting Individual Needs of Ringers*

1. *Giving extra help*: Handbell ringing is a coordination of musical skill with motor ability, and in every choir the ringers' abilities will vary. Some ringers will be very happy to handle just one bell while others will want to handle at least

---

* For a more detailed treatment of the effective use of the *Cambridge Quarters*, see *A letter from The Handbell Choir Loft*, Vol. I, No. 1, September 1958, pp. 3-5.

two. In some instances it will be necessary for the director to have special sessions with a ringer. This is especially true when there is a wide age span in the handbell choir.

The two problems most usually faced are technical skill in ringing and memorization of music. In the latter instance the director can either say the words in the rhythm of the music or play the complete handbell score on the piano while the ringer either rings, or pretends to ring, his bell or bells. For further help, the director can both play the score and say the words. (See Chapter Six, Section V, 2, which deals with the "how" of memorization.) In private sessions with the teacher the ringer will gain the ability and confidence to keep up with the rest of the choir.

2. *Giving more difficult rings to those who can handle them*: Insofar as possible the director will want to keep the more capable ringers challenged. For example, in the event of a trill which involves notes usually played by two different ringers, the director will choose the ringer with the better motor ability to ring the trill. The four-bell ring is another challenge for the more advanced ringers. (See Chapter Three, Section II, 17 and 18, which deal with these rings.)

3. *Encouraging experimentation*: Those ringers who have creative minds, and those who like to spend extra time after rehearsals, sometimes discover new rings or bell effects. A director will want to encourage this kind of experimentation, giving guidance where necessary.

Some ringers become enthusiastic enough about the hand-bell choir to want to write music for the group to play. A director can encourage individual ringers in creative work by assigning a simple tune and suggesting that each ringer who is willing harmonize it in a different fashion. In advanced creative work it could be further suggested that they emulate the style of a certain composer.*

IV. *Directing*

1. *The director as conductor*: Just as it is advisable to have the director of a singing choir conduct the rehearsals and performances, it is also advisable to have the director conduct the handbell choir from a position in front of the group. This position, especially when the choir is ringing from memory, gives him the maximum amount of control in dynamic shading, in precision ringing, and more particularly in helping a ringer who misses a ring or rings at the wrong time.

It is a responsibility of every director to be so thoroughly familiar with the music that at any time during a performance given by memory he can aid a ringer whose memory fails. This the director can do by looking and pointing at the ringer when he is to ring the next time and continuing to do this until he senses that the person who "blanked out" has recovered his memory.

As well as helping the ringer who made the error, the director should point at the ringer or ringers whose bells are to be played after the omitted note or notes. This gives confidence to those ringers who have not heard the note they expected to hear, thus preserving the musical pattern and the morale of the group. It is especially necessary for the director to give this kind of help when a single melodic line is being rung. When the arrangement is harmonic, the director should give particular attention to the melodic line. When the director

---

* One director assigned the tune "Twinkle, Twinkle, Little Star" and had two members of the bell choir harmonize it in the style of two composers; *e.g.*, Bach and Mozart. A third ringer arranged it in a modern idiom, calling it "Go, You Crazy Star."

is alert, the omission of a note is often not detected by the audience.

In chart or manuscript ringing it is much more difficult for the director to have control. However, in chart ringing the director can point to the notes, focusing the attention of the entire bell choir.

2. *The director as participant*: Many groups have had considerable success in having the director participate as one of the ringers. Usually he is placed at one end of the group where he is easily visible to the others. Often when this is the case, charts or small music on a table or stands are used almost exclusively. The tempo is set by a nod of the head or the beat of a hand.

V. *Training a Second Bell Choir*

1. *To provide substitute ringers*: There should be a definite system established for providing substitutes both for rehearsals and performances. Some directors have been successful in having one or two substitute ringers available when needed, persons who are talented musically but cannot make regular rehearsals or feel they cannot devote enough time to a mastery of the complete repertoire.

If a ringer knows he is going to have certain specific conflicts during the year, especially for performances, he himself should find a musical person who will be willing to substitute and attend as many rehearsals as are necessary to perfect the music. If a ringer, regardless of his value to the group, is not willing to assume this responsibility for his assigned note or notes he should be dropped completely, or used as a regular substitute.

A more adequate way of dealing with the usual problem of necessary absences is to have two choirs working on identical repertoire.

In order to provide substitute ringers through a second choir, the director should try to keep the same pattern for the division of bells for the two groups. For example, if one ringer is handling the low G and A bells in the first group, the same pattern of division should hold for the second group with one ringer covering the same low G and A. Each ringer should know who plays his bell or bells in the other choir and should have his telephone number readily available on the inside cover of his music. In the event that a ringer must miss a rehearsal, he should be directly responsible for having his substitute present for that rehearsal. If a ringer must be absent from a performance he should contact not only his substitute but also the director. The director will know if the substitute will need any extra help, and will take care of any problem accordingly.*

2. *To be a feeder group*: It is good to draw from the personnel of the second choir when new ringers are needed in the first choir. (See Chapter Seven, Section III, which deals with the selection of ringers.) However, occasionally there will be a musically talented person who because of age and ability should go directly into the first choir.

3. *To absorb all who are interested*: In a church with a multiple choir program it is usually essential to have at least two ringing choirs to absorb all those who are interested.

4. *To perform*: There are many demands placed upon a handbell choir. (Refer to Chapter One, Section I, which deals with the role of the handbell choir.) A second choir can gain

---

* For several directors' different approaches to this problem of absenteeism, see *A letter from The Handbell Choir Loft, op. cit.,* pp. 1-3.

valuable experience by taking some of the engagements. This puts less pressure on the first choir.

5. *To take care of some of the mechanics of the program*: Some directors who have enough ringers for two choirs simply divide the ringers into two groups. Each group or choir has its own repertoire or the two choirs can work on similar repertoire. (See this chapter, Section V, 1, which deals with the advantage of similar repertoire.) While one group is ringing the other group can prepare charts and duplicator masters or mimeograph stencils for reproducing individual music,* take care of the musical library, take turns directing, or learn to listen critically.

---

* The preparation of charts (See Chapter Six, Section I, 3, which deals with this subject) and individual music is time-consuming. It takes considerable practice to do a good job. Young people could be trained to relieve the director of this problem; but until they become skilled, the director would have to have considerable patience.

For reproducing individual arrangements, the spirit duplicator is found to be easier to use than a mimeograph machine. The masters are less expensive than stencils and much simpler to prepare.

CHAPTER SIX

Methods of Learning and Performing

I.   *The Chart (See Figure 7, page 53.)*

1. *Uses*:

A. For beginners: In working with a beginning group the director will want to be able to focus the attention of the ringers, especially when there are ringers who do not understand musical notation. The chart is an answer to this problem. The chart is either held by the director in his left hand or placed on a stand. In using the chart the director points to the notes with his finger or with the eraser end of a pencil, clearly indicating the rhythm with his arm. Before beginning any number, the director should set the tempo by counting at least a measure, and should conclude his counting with such words as "Ready, play," spoken in rhythm. For example, if a number begins on the fourth and last beat of the measure, the director would begin by saying in strict rhythm: "One, two, three, four, one, ready, play." The director will be able to tell when charts are no longer necessary.

B. For music incorporating new rings: When a new ring is being introduced to a handbell choir it is wise to use a chart for the number which incorporates this new ring. This centers the ringers' attention and makes the new ring easier to explain.

C.   For short responses during a service: Usually when a bell choir rings responses during a service it is not visible to the congregation. They may ring from the balcony or the narthex. In either situation charts are often a help.

D. In performance: Many choirs use charts in performance with considerable success. However, in church ringing,

Figure 7

charts present several drawbacks. Visually, chart ringing is not as attractive as ringing from memory. This is especially true when several numbers are being played, necessitating a juggling of charts in view of the congregation. Also, in many parts of the church auditorium lighting is inadequate. Further, during special services lights are often dimmed in the middle of a handbell performance — sometimes without warning. If charts are used, the person in charge of lighting should be made aware of the times at which the bells are to be rung. Also, musically there is less control over precision ringing and dynamic shading when charts are used; however, when covering more repertoire is a major consideration, especially in adult ringing choirs, charts are a decided advantage.

E. For demonstrations and lectures: During lectures and demonstrations, bell charts can be used to show the audience or the workshop examples of handbell music.

F. For publicity: Pictures of charts or ringers reading from charts make colorful publicity.

2. *Materials*: White poster paper, which usually comes size 22" x 28", can be procured at any stationery store. Most directors use black India ink for making the chart. Some directors use various colors of paper and/or ink. A few directors with small choirs use a different color of ink for each ringer's part. Flat Speedball penpoints of various sizes are used in drawing. Especially useful and recommended are C-5 for the staves; C-3 for clefs, key and time signatures, words and rests; and C-0 for the notes. By holding penpoint C-0 on the side, straight stems and flags can be made. The large surface of the C-0 point makes it easy to outline the main body of the note and to fill it in quickly when it needs to be.

Instead of poster paper, white window shades can be used and placed on a frame which has hooks to hold them open. Rolled shades are not as adaptable in performance as poster paper charts which do not need to be mounted, but they are more easily transported and stored. If chart ringing is to be done exclusively in performance it might be worth procuring a frame which would hold several shades, and each could be lowered and secured to the bottom of the frame as needed.

3. *Procedure for making a chart*: Each penpoint to be used should have a separate penholder. The poster paper is placed on newspapers on a table or on the floor. A yardstick is needed for making the staves. The approximate number of staves must be thought through and adequate space must be left between each staff to accommodate leger lines and words. The staves are drawn first. To prevent smearing, the point of the pen must be held at such an angle that it cannot contact the edge of the ruler that rests on the paper. The ink must be dry before proceeding. Point C-5 will not be used again and should be placed in a glass of water to prevent hardening of the ink. When the chart has been completed all the penpoints should be removed from the water and wiped clean or placed on a blotter until stored.

A light pencil line can be drawn under each staff as a guide line for the words, placing it far enough below the staff so as not to crowd notes requiring leger lines. Light vertical guide lines can be used to get notes of chords in proper position.

Next, take penpoint C-3 and put in the caption of the chart and the clef, key and time signature of the first staff. From then on, to prevent smearing, work measure by measure, alternating penpoints C-3 and C-0 as needed.

Another way to make charts quickly, although not as attractive or accurately detailed as the penpoint method, is to use a Magic Marker or black felt marking pen. Either of these can be procured at a good stationery store. The Magic Marker is considerably more reasonable than the felt marking pen and does just as good a job. A black china marker pencil can also be used, but in placing the charts one against another the markings would eventually become smeared unless sprayed with a fixative coating such as used in protecting charcoal or pastel sketches.*

Some directors use round gummed seals for the quarter notes, saving a considerable amount of time. Although round quarter notes are not true to form, they are legible. These are a special help when several people are working on a chart, as it keeps a majority of the notes uniform. The round seals come gummed and self-moistened, the latter type being the more convenient. They can be obtained in almost any good stationery store.

II. *The Blackboard*

In encouraging experimentation the blackboard is an indispensable aid. If a ringer, or several ringers working together, find an interesting combination of tones and various ways of producing them, these can be jotted down on a blackboard and used as a further basis for experimentation. Also, some directors will want to encourage original composition. These numbers can all be placed on a blackboard to be subject to the analysis and criticism of all the ringers. (See Chapter Five, Section III, 3, which deals with encouraging experimentation.)

III. *Rote or Melody Line Ringing*

In this method of learning the director points out the melody by indicating to each ringer when to play. No music is used,

---

* Krylon Fixatif Crystal Clear (No. 1306A) dries in seconds and can be procured at most art stores.

leaving the burden of responsibility on the director. Through repetition the ringing becomes smooth and meaningful.

As well as being good for simple melodic line this system can be used for doubling the melodic line. To do this, each ringer must know who rings the handbell an octave from his. The two ringers who have the bells an octave apart could be considered partners. As the director points to each of the ringers playing a melodic note his partner can also ring, but only if the director indicates through some signal that the melody should be doubled.

A good way to vary a number done with melody alone is to have part of it done with simple melodic line, ending with the last phrase or phrases doubled. This procedure can be followed only when the last phrase or phrases lie within a range of bells where the melody can be doubled in a consistent relationship; *i.e.,* either the octave or an octave below.

Another way to vary melodic line ringing (when the range of notes involved permits) is to ring the second of two similar phrases an octave below or above the original or first phrase. (See "Angels We Have Heard on High.")

This technique of melody line ringing with all of its variations can be used to build up a program quickly. (See Chapter Eleven, which deals with program planning.) The simple tune should be interspersed with the more elaborate arrangements of music. Actually, a simple melody can be worked out sufficiently for performance by just going through it two or three times.

This technique is very rewarding for the first session with beginning ringers because it produces results so quickly. The director may want to have others in the group try pointing out a simple melody, either in a first session or later, in order to determine a ringer's musicianship or directing ability. It is lots of fun, also, to have different ringers try to point out a melody or create an interesting tonal pattern. The director can ring the bell or bells of the person who is the temporary director.

IV. *Individual Music and Ways to Hold It*

There is no substitute for each ringer's having his own music. He uses it in rehearsal as well as during the week in private practice. During rehearsal the music is held on his lap. When music is used during a performance, such as for an anthem, it is similarly held or can be placed on a music stand, on the music rack of a choir stall, or on the top of the organ console when the ringers are standing around it. (See Chapter Ten, Section I, which suggests various positions the choir can assume during a service of worship.) Usually entire anthems are too difficult to memorize, so ringers should be granted the same privilege as singers in the use of music. Similarly, ringers should not be expected to memorize lengthy compositions for organ and handbells.

When choirs use individual music for both rehearsal and performance, some directors have a special long stand built which will hold the music of all the ringers. It must be high enough so that the ringers can see comfortably as they stand behind it. It can be constructed in one or two sections for good portability and it can be straight across or slightly curved.

Ringers should be encouraged to circle notes they are to ring, or circle the word or number on which they play, or otherwise mark their individual music so it will be easy to ring or memorize. If a ringer has two basic tones assigned he may want to circle with two different colors and use other colors for accidentals. If keeping colored pencils available is not convenient, another way a ringer can help himself if he rings two bells is to use a single line for one bell and a double line for the other.

Some directors find that it saves rehearsal time to mark each ringer's music with colors or some other system of marking before issuing new music. However, this is extra work for the director and prevents the ringer from getting the experience of reading the music and finding his notes for himself. Also it is good to consider that some ringers can read the music easily with no mark whatsoever or just a pencil mark circling or underlining the words or chords to be played. The better way to save rehearsal time is to issue the music a week before using it in rehearsal; then the ringer can mark it the way he finds best for himself.

V. *Memorization*

1. *Why*: When a bell choir plays from memory the director has more control over the precision and dynamic shading of the ringing. Also, ringers will be able to assume various formations when necessary without having to focus attention on a chart. For example, a choir may have to ring from pews in a balcony or on church steps, and in so doing may have to form two or three rows instead of the usual horseshoe formation.

When problems of lighting are a consideration, again memorization is mandatory. Such problems arise when there is dim lighting in a church, when the group is doing outdoor ringing at night, or when they ring under the bright lights of television, newsreel or stage work.

For processionals and parades, handbell music must be memorized. The only exception to this is when there are enough ringers so that each ringer holds only one bell apiece, or so that one of the ringers in a double line has a free hand. Then music can be held. Holding music, however, detracts from freedom in ringing and the majestic appearance of the processing choir. In a dire emergency it is conceivable that music could be attached to the back of the preceding ringer or to the sleeve of the ringer himself. This method is not desirable and could be tolerated, if at all, only as a last resort.

Unity in performance is an important result of memorization. By the time the music is memorized, the choir has learned to think, play, and even breathe together as a unit.

2. *How*: In all handbell music which is to be memorized each chord (or note) is given a word or a syllable of the original text, or a number. (See the *Book of Handbell Music, Set I*.) The ringer can circle either the word or chord or both in which his note appears. (See Section IV of this chapter.) This music he uses in rehearsal and takes home for further work. The ringer can practice without bells by saying the words and numbers in the rhythm of the music. While doing this, he thinks through the words, syllables of words, and numbers on which his bell or bells are rung. If he needs to practice ringing technique he can use any object as a bell to practice the arm and wrist movement, "ringing" at the times his notes appear.

In rehearsal the director can aid the choir in group memorization. After playing a number through completely with the music, the director gives the members two or three minutes to study the first phrase of music. As each ringer knows his part he turns his music over, and when all the music is turned, the director then has the group play the first phrase from memory. He then gives the ringers another few seconds to check up on any mistakes. Again they play the phrase, repeating the procedure until perfection is attained. They then proceed to study the next phrase. However, instead of playing just the new phrase, it is usually better to ring the number from the beginning. This takes only a few seconds longer and insures the group against forgetting the first part of a number while working on the new phrase.

With proper concentration, it usually takes only a small part of the rehearsal hour to memorize an entire number. The ringers need take only a few minutes to review each day to keep the music well in mind before the next rehearsal, when more can be done in precision and dynamic shading.

When a choir does a great deal of memory work the director should assign the music several months in advance, whenever possible.

CHAPTER SEVEN

The "How" of Organization

I. *The Relationship of the Handbell Choir to the Total Church Program*

1. *Through the ministry of music*: One way to include the handbell choir program in the total educational life of the church is to organize it as a part of the larger choir system. In doing this, there are three ways to instigate the bell choir rehearsals. These methods demand of new ringers that they maintain faithful membership in a singing choir.

A. Initial handbell rehearsals as a part of a singing choir rehearsal: The director of the handbell choirs, especially if he is also the director of the singing choirs, will want to bring the bells to the singing choir rehearsals and demonstrate very simply during a few rehearsals the characteristic tone and uses of the handbell. These demonstrations should be brief, and vary from week to week, giving members some opportunity to handle and ring the bells. After two or three weeks, when the director detects a certain excitement about handbells, he should then be ready to announce the first handbell choir rehearsal, inviting all to share in this new, dynamic experience. Whenever possible, the bell choir rehearsals should either precede or follow the regular singing choir rehearsals to prevent singers and ringers from overcrowding busy schedules.

B. Handbell rehearsals as a part of singing choir rehearsals: Some directors have used handbells in all their singing choir rehearsals. This could happen only if the singing choir rehearses no less than two hours. In adult choir rehearsals the bell ringing could be kept to a minimal half hour, while the younger choirs, who usually have fewer vocal demands, could use an hour of the rehearsal time for bells.

Some musical numbers could be worked out jointly with bells and voices. However, a big detriment to this method of scheduling would be the problem of absorbing all the singers into the ringing choir, as well as finding within a two-hour span adequate time for both ringing and singing. The singers in a church are real ministers to a congregation, and the quality of their contribution should never be sacrificed for the sake of using handbells effectively. An advantage of a combination method is that all those who contribute to the music of the church have the pleasure and challenge of ringing bells without an additional demand on their time.

C. Initial handbell rehearsals as separate rehearsals, but drawing from members of the singing choirs: The director may want to begin his bell choir program with one large organizational meeting to which he has invited another bell choir to come and demonstrate ringing, or for which he himself has prepared an inspirational presentation. All singing choir members should be urged to attend; and at the close of the session, all those who are interested should be asked to sign up. From this list he can determine how many handbell choirs should be formed. As nearly as possible, he will keep the ringers coming on the same day that they come for singing choir rehearsal. This practice assures the director that the people who have signed up will probably have no conflicts in their schedules regarding any of the rehearsals.

If a director in looking over his program finds that he will have to have one afternoon or evening devoted exclusively to all the handbell rehearsals, it is wise to have the organizational meeting at that same time, and to explain to those attending that this will be the time for the handbell choir rehearsals. This assures a valid sign-up list. (See this chapter, Section I, 3, A and B, which deal with suggestions for the one-day and two-day rehearsal systems.)

2. *Through youth organizations*: Some churches which limit ringing to the youth of the church find it best to organize through the educational program of the church, giving priority for membership in the handbell choir to those whose records indicate the most faithful participation in the Church School, the Fellowships or other groups. This approach has two advantages. It attracts those who might have difficulty in becoming members of a singing choir, such as boys whose voices are changing, or those who have never been a part of a singing choir. This system also tends to strengthen the organizations from which the ringers are drawn, because of the special dedication the ringers must have both to the new choir and to the original organization of which they are members.

In working through some larger program the rehearsals can be planned as an integral part of that program, or at some other time during the week. (See suggestions in the following section for programming.)

3. *As an independent organization*: A handbell choir which is organized as a completely separate and new program in the church eventually attracts new people to the church. Perhaps the director would want to work through the choirs or other organizations initially, but later he could accept non-church members. These new ringers may become church members.

A busy handbell choir tends to attract friends of ringers, and soon the director will find he has a waiting list. When an individual exhibits great interest in ringing by attending rehearsals just to observe, it is good practice after a period of time for the director to try to absorb that individual into the choir. Perhaps for a while he would ring one of the bells which is used only occasionally, or he could be used to ring an accidental or two that might occur in a number. Then when the director needs a new ringer, he has one all trained and eager.

Another idea employed by some directors to absorb new-comers or those who might feel inferior musically, is to use them as "keepers of the bells." A choir can easily use two such people to be generally useful to the choir and the director. Usually these assistants are well disciplined in the routine of the choir through their association with the choir, and eventually, when the opportunity comes, make fine ringers.

A. The one-day rehearsal system: The director can easily handle one, two or three one-hour bell rehearsals in an afternoon. It is wise to plan adequate regular rehearsals rather than to rely on extra rehearsals to perfect a performance. A weekly rehearsal is usually adequate. (A few directors have had success with bi-weekly rehearsals.) The day of rehearsal depends on the church and community program. There can be either an afternoon or evening devoted to the handbell choirs.

B. The two-day rehearsal system: Because a handbell choir program is something very special and demands people who are willing to put this activity first, it is often desirable to have two rehearsals a week thus strengthening the choir or choirs. Two weekly rehearsals are especially helpful in the first year of ringing, and could be a requirement for the best ringers, having a second bell choir rehearse only once a week. The two-day system gives more opportunity for creativity and experimentation.

Another way of conducting the two-day rehearsal system is to have the more experienced handbell choir rehearse on one day with the less experienced choir rehearsing on the other. The ringer who is newly accepted in the first bell choir would be required to continue in the second bell choir for the period of a year or some other suitable span of time. This extra training widens the experience of the newly promoted ringer. Both rehearsals can be an hour; but better results are obtained when the more experienced group has between an hour and a half and two hours, with a small break for refreshments or business.

II. *The Importance of the Press*

In initiating a handbell choir program it is essential to get good press coverage. It is a special event to have handbells come to a church. The bell choir brings new light and vitality to Christian worship. The music of the bell is exhilarating, and there should be an air of expectancy over the event of the use of handbells in the service of worship.

There are three points at which ample press coverage is desirable: when a handbell choir visits the church which desires to have its own handbell choirs; when the bells actually arrive and rehearsals begin; and when the bell choirs are ready to contribute significantly to worship.

III. *The Selection of Ringers*

1. *The use of examinations*: Some directors who have more than enough ringers for one choir use tests to determine the qualifications of potential ringers. It is good to have these qualifying examinations *after* the first few handbell choir rehearsals. This plan gives everyone, regardless of musical training or lack of it, an equal chance to learn something about the

fundamentals of reading music and the art of ringing. Potential ringers who do not make the first choir can either be used as substitutes or can be the nucleus of a second choir. (See Chapter Five, Section V, which deals with the training of a second bell choir.) Testing is a fairly sure procedure for securing good new ringers, providing the testing measures the aspiring ringer's physical coordination in actually ringing the bell, his general knowledge of the fundamentals of music, his sense of rhythm, and his ability to memorize, if memorization is to be a part of the program. (See Chapter Six, Section V, which deals with memorization.) Occasionally a fine musician will not be able to master the arm and wrist movement necessary for consistently good ringing.

A. The three major parts of the examination: In a good examination there should be at least three major parts spreading over at least two handbell choir rehearsals. One part should be written and deal with the simple fundamental musical symbols that are used in bell ringing. This part of the examination should deal only with the material that has been covered in class sessions.

1.) Written: Keep in mind when preparing the examination that all musical facts appearing in the testing must have first been presented clearly during prior rehearsals, with ample time for clearing up questions. The following sample of a written examination should be graded on the basis of one hundred per cent:

Name .... Date ....

Identify the following symbols:

(To each successive symbol a new symbol is added
and is to be identified.)

1. ..... 2. ..... 3. ..... 4. ..... 5. ..... 6. .....

Identify the handbell ring of each note or chord:

7. .... 8. .... 9. .... 10. ....

Fill in the blanks:

11. 4 3 2 and 2 are called .... signatures.
     4, 4, 2   4

12. ♩ is a .... note.

13. 𝅗𝅥 is a .... note.

14. ♪ is a .... note.

15. 𝅗𝅥 is a .... note.

16. How many scores of music are in the following box?

Answer: ....

68

Name the following notes (Give the letter-name):

17. .... 18. .... 19. .... 20. ....

Have you studied any musical instrument other than bells? ....

What instrument or instruments? ....

How long? ....

2.) Sight-Reading: The second part of the testing should deal with sight-reading. This gives the director a chance to analyze muscular coordination and rhythm as well as ability to read the notes. Each ringer has a separate turn and should be alone with the director so that he has a minimum of distraction. He should either read from a chart or from individual handbell music.

For the actual test the director should select a piece of music which is not too simple and yet not far beyond the skill of the majority of his ringers. Then the director should select a handbell part (a tone) which occurs a minimum of 20 to 25 times and which provides some variety in the specific rings; i.e., straight, back, roll, etc. Each person taking the test should read the same part, as this provides the director with a basis for evaluation. When the ringer comes to the testing room he should bring with him one of the bells he usually rings. The bell he rings will undoubtedly not be the tone chosen for the testing, but for special rings and even straight rings, the ringer will find his own bell more comfortable to handle. Thus he is put more at ease for the test. Also, by bringing his own assigned handbell the ringer has no prior knowledge of the part he will be required to read.

The director should play the number through on the piano, simultaneously saying the words and numbers aloud so that the ringer gets as much help as possible. If using a piano is not convenient and the director uses a very familiar tune, he could just read the words and numbers in the correct rhythm. The ringer can pretend to ring this first time through, but the second time through the director should keep track of the errors, and then grade the ringer on the basis of one hundred per cent.

3.) Memorization: The third part of the testing should have to do with memorization. The director should issue the same piece of music to all the ringers at the first testing session. He should assign the same handbell part to each of the potential ringers. Then the director should acquaint them with the music by playing it through on the piano, together with reading the words and numbers. The following week, having taken the music home to practice, the ringers should be given the chance to ring the bell part, each ringer demonstrating privately with the director his skill at memorization. This part of the testing should be graded on the basis of one hundred per cent.

B. Grading the examination: The three grades from the three parts of the testing should be averaged, and the twelve ringers with the highest score taken into the first bell choir. (See Chapter Four, Sections I and II, which deal with the formation of the choir.) The fact that the three grades are averaged recognizes the importance of the three facets of the testing. Further, it gives the ringers with their individual strengths and weaknesses equal opportunity. If there is a tie for the twelfth place in the choir the director should choose the ringer with the higher score in memorization, as this score is an indication not only of ability to memorize but the conscientiousness of a potential ringer to take home assignments seriously.

If a director eventually wants two handbell choirs but does not have enough ringers, those with the lowest scores in the first choir could also be required to ring with the second choir until enough new ringers could be secured to form two complete choirs. This double service strengthens the weaker ringers in the first choir. Ringers doing such double service should ring the same bell or bells in the second choir as they ring in the first.

2. *The use of past attendance records*: Some directors place the highest value on the potential ringer's singing choir record or some other church record, considering faithfulness, discipline and overall cooperation. This system coupled with some testing gives the person who has not had the opportunity for musical education equal opportunity with the musical person. Often a person who has had no previous musical experience makes a capable ringer. Latent musical talents or an innate rhythmical sense may be discovered. Couple these abilities with good powers of concentration, another necessity for good performance, and the director has the necessary material to mold into an expert ringer.

3. *The value of the potential ringer's attitude*: Both of the above criteria (testing and past record of faithfulness) should be employed when selecting a first handbell choir. Even more important, however, is the spirit of the ringer and his desire to become an able member of a ringing choir. At the beginning of the church year the ringer and the ringer's parents, when the ringer is a young person, must realize that if he accepts a place in the handbell choir *the commitment is for the entire year,* plus, insofar as possible, any activities that might be planned through the summer vacation months. Sometimes this calls for a sacrifice of personal plans for the sake of the group.

4. *Importance of parental attitude*: In considering ringers through high school age, the director should have some personal contact with the parents so that they become familiar with the goals and problems inherent in working with handbell choirs.

Parents should know the importance placed on each ringer in the choir. A handbell choir is only as strong as its weakest ringer. Perfect attendance must be the goal of each person and assignments must be done faithfully. Parents should be familiar with any system worked out by the director for substitute ringers. (See Chapter V, Section V, 1, which deals with some possible suggestions for providing substitute ringers.)

During busy handbell seasons such as Christmas and Easter, parents should realize that there may be occasional extra rehearsals as well as extra performances. This fact may affect family holiday plans.

The director will want to know about the general health of potential ringers as well as something about his grades in school. It is not wise for the director to accept a ringer who may have to cut out all extra-curricular activities because of low grades in school.

There are various ways of reaching parents and attempting to secure their allegiance. The director may find telephone calls or personal visitations in the home the best way to reach parents. Some directors have found it advisable to hold a meeting with all parents of those who want to become bell ringers. Together with the minister of the church, the director explains the purpose of the choir and the needs peculiar to a sound handbell choir program. At such a meeting refreshments should be served to create a relaxed atmosphere and there should be ample time for questions and answers. Parents who understand the functioning of a choir will give greater support to the total program.

CHAPTER EIGHT

The First Rehearsal

I. *Purpose*

The primary purpose of the first session with new ringers should be to inspire them to full allegiance to the handbell program. The director should plan his opening remarks carefully. He should have a plan in hand so that the first rehearsal moves along quickly, interspersed with interesting background material about tower bells and handbells.* The director should select data about which he himself is the most excited, and the high pitch of this interest will carry through to the new ringers, provided imagination is used in the presentation.

Probably not all the material in this chapter can be used in the first rehearsal. Some of it can be used in subsequent sessions and indeed, some suggestions, such as scale ringing and ringing changes referred to in Section VII, may be used regularly in future rehearsals.

II. *Demonstration of Tone*

First of all, the ringers will be interested in seeing, hearing and ringing the handbells. A good procedure is to have the bells on a table for this first rehearsal so that all can see. An impor-

---

* There have been a number of books on the subject of bells published in England. Almost any one of these deals briefly with handbells. For a more comprehensive treatment of the subject of handbells as well as a bibliography with a partial listing of English as well as American books see *The Story Of Handbells* by Scott Brink Parry, Whittemore Associates, Inc. of Boston, Mass.; 1957. As this book does not cover the story of church handbell ringing, except for an occasional reference, the reader should see the history that appears in Section III of this chapter.

tant part of the presentation is to impress on the ringers' minds the value of the bells. Not only should the cost of the bells be considered, but more importantly, the ringers should be told how long it took for the set to arrive as well as the fact that it is not easy to replace a cracked bell should one be dropped. Because it usually takes several months to complete the process of reordering and replacing a cracked handbell,* most directors when working with young people have the bells placed on the floor at all times, except for the brief demonstration during this first rehearsal.

The director will want to illustrate the difference in tone as the mouth of the bell is held in different positions at the completion of a straight ring, having the ringers discover for themselves that when the mouth of the bell tilts back too far at the close of a ring the tone is softer and can become lost in a chord when all the other ringers hold the mouth of the bell more upright. (See Chapter Three, Section II, 1, which deals with the straight ring.)

The director will also want to demonstrate some of the special rings, having various members of the group try them. Throughout this part of the presentation he will want to impress on the minds of the ringers the importance of keeping hands off the metal, especially if gloves are not to be worn when ringing. Not only do fingermarks discolor the bell, but they can eventually corrode the metal and distort the tone of the bell. To prevent any damage that might occur when fingers accidentally come in contact with the metal it is necessary to rub the metal after each rehearsal with a soft cloth. If a cloth or flannel bags (see Chapter Two, Sections II and III, which deal with the use of

---

* The best way to order one or a small number of bells, is to send an airmail letter directly to the foundry. Request that the order be sent by parcel post just as soon as possible, stating your reason for urgency.

flannel bags and polishing) are not readily available the ringers can rub the bells on skirts or trousers until all fingerprints are removed and the high luster of the bells is restored. Bells should be rubbed occasionally even when gloves are worn.

III. *History of Handbell Choirs*

1. *The ringing band and handbell choir defined*: A ringing band is a group of handbell ringers whose interests embrace all kinds of music: secular, popular, folk, classical and carols, and often the field of English change ringing. A band may be a privately organized group of adults or young people, or it may be organized through a school or community group.

A handbell choir is a group of handbell ringers whose musical activities are largely confined to the church and to ringing religious music. A choir may appear in functions that are not religious in themselves and may on special occasions ring any kind of music, but a handbell choir never loses its identification with the church.

2. *The development of ringing bands in America*: In the 1850's a boy named Arthur H. Nichols helped the sexton chime the eight bells in the tower of the Old North Church, in Boston, for Sunday service. Later, after hearing the change ringing in England and becoming interested in that science, Dr. Nichols was delighted to discover that the bells in the Old North Church which had been sent over from England in 1745 were originally hung for change ringing in the English manner. He also found records showing there had been an early band of change ringers of which Paul Revere was a member. Dr. Nichols arranged to have the bells rehung. He found seven English change ringers around Boston who, with the addition of his daughter Margaret,

now Mrs. Arthur Shurcliff, were able to form a band. Mrs. Shurcliff became the first woman in this country skilled in the art.

In 1902 she discovered in England the small, perfectly tuned handbells upon which English bell ringers practice change ringing. While in England she rang two peals on handbells in one day. The owner of the bells was so impressed that he gave them to her. On her return to Boston, finding tune ringing more popular than change ringing, Mrs. Schurcliff ordered a larger set of bells and with her children rang carols on Beacon Hill on Christmas Eve. Listeners were soon writing her to find out how to obtain bells and they have been writing her ever since.*

3. *The beginnings of the church handbell choir*: During the Second World War, Dr. Paul Austin Wolfe, minister of The Brick Presbyterian Church, New York City, heard a ringing band in the Adirondacks. He decided to make use of handbells in the church. In 1944 he ordered a set of handbells which did not arrive, because of war time restrictions, until 1947. On Christmas Eve of that same year, some young people at The Brick Church rang a few carols, establishing an annual custom, and thus bringing handbells to the service of worship.

Although there had been, during the early part of this century, two or three groups of bell ringers which were initiated by workers in churches,** The Brick Church Bell Ringers is

---

* For more detailed accounts of this story see *Overtones*, Vol. 2, Nos 1 and 3, January and July 1956, and Vol. 4, No. 3, May 1958.

** Margaret Shurcliff had in her ringing band Leland Arnold, organist at Newton, Massachusetts; Mrs. Norman Erb, director of Christian Education at Old South Church of Boston, organized a ringing band in 1930; and The Rev. Paul Wesley Bare in 1932 founded in Pennsylvania the American Alps Swiss Handbell Quartet, a group of four men performing on 32 bells. He also organized a similar women's group. (See Chapter Two, *The Story Of Handbells* by Parry.)

believed to be the first ringing choir concerned with the integral use of ringing and singing in a liturgical service of worship.*

The Rev. Paul Freed, a former assistant minister at The Brick Church, carried the handbell choir idea with him when he became minister of The College Hill Presbyterian Church in Easton, Pennsylvania. There in 1949 Mr. Freed introduced a young man by the name of Scott Parry to these handbells and asked him to organize a handbell choir. It was this bell choir that joined The Brick Church Bell Ringers in ringing for the General Assembly of The Presbyterian Church, which in 1952 met in New York City for the first time in over fifty years. This joint performance introduced handbell choirs to Presbyterian churches all over the country.

In 1951, Dr. Wolfe asked the writer to develop and strengthen the handbell choir at The Brick Church. This was done by making the handbell choir a regular part of the singing choir program and exploring its many possibilities for use in Christian worship.

It was shortly after this that The Brick Church Bell Ringers appeared on national television,** in movie and television news-reel films, on a C.B.S. Church of the Air broadcast, and for two consecutive Christmas seasons with the New York Philharmonic. Another high point was the performance of the bell ringers and youth choir for three years at the Candlelight Carol Service at Union Theological Seminary in New York City.

Throughout the country organists and choir directors were catching the vision of what handbell choirs could do for wor-

---

* "Bell choirs of handbell ringers are becoming popular in churches. There are said to be around 100 already. The first one it is believed was organized at The Brick Presbyterian Church in 1947."
— *Saturday Evening Post*, December 22, 1956
** The first national program was the Garry Moore show on December 22, 1953.

ship, and even more importantly, what they could do to capture the loyalties of the youth of the church. The idea "snowballed" rapidly until now there are handbell choirs in churches small and large in all sections of the United States.

4. *National organizations and festivals*: In March of 1954 The First Church Handbell Festival was held at The College Hill Presbyterian Church of Easton, Pennsylvania, under the leadership of The Rev. Paul Freed, with the musical program under the leadership of the writer. A ringers' banquet, a dance, and rehearsal time for massed numbers highlighted the Saturday program; and the Sunday culmination was the service of worship which took place in an overflowing church. This was the beginning of a movement which has taken place annually and which has grown from three participating choirs to well over ten.

In June of that same year, Mrs. Arthur Shurcliff invited some members of the American Carillon Association in Boston to meet with the members of the New England Guild of English Handbell Ringers at her home to ring bells. It was at that meeting that the American Guild of English Handbell Ringers was organized, with Mrs. Shurcliff as the first president. In August of 1954 the first festival was held at Castle Hill, Ipswich, Massachusetts, a large estate which each year lends its charm to the handbell enthusiasts who attend the three-day convocation of classes, workshops, concerts, beach parties and tours.

5. *National publications*:*

A. *Overtones*: This is the official organ of the American Guild of English Handbell Ringers. It is usually published four times a year. It contains feature articles about various

---

* *Overtones*: Mrs. Norman Erb, 1661 Crescent Place, N.W., Washington 9, D. C.; *A letter from The Handbell Choir Loft*: 41 Bayview Place, Staten Island 4, New York; *Choristers' Guild*: Box 211, Santa Barbara, California.

ringing bands and choirs; news of note concerning individual choirs, festivals and workshops; advertisements concerning books, records and music; as well as some ringing suggestions of general interest to bands and choirs. It is the general clearing ground for any information pertaining to handbells.

B. *A letter from The Handbell Choir Loft*: This is a letter which goes out to ministers and musicians who have or are contemplating having a handbell choir program. It was conceived at a planning meeting for The Fourth Annual Church Handbell Festival and it is written by church leaders for church leaders. It is published four times a year, each issue dealing with a specific problem or plan for the church leader as well as regular features including the arranging of music, the use of handbells in worship, a problem box, and announcements of unusual church events, festivals and workshops. Each issue contains some church music or repertoire suggestions.

C. *Choristers' Guild Letters*: This is a letter which deals with the problems faced by the director of young people's singing choirs, and from time to time this interesting paper for the church musician contains information for the director of the handbell choir.

6. *Ringing for international audiences*: In the spring of 1956 the ringing of church music was brought to twenty-seven different countries, and the vocal text of the anthem used was translated into fifteen languages by the Voice of America films. Again the following year this same choir, The West Side Presbyterian Handbell Choir of Ridgewood, New Jersey, was heard and seen around the world through the same medium.

IV. *Arrangement of Ringers*

After the first part of the presentation, which should take ten minutes or so, everyone will be eager to ring. The director will then want to line up his group quickly, taller ringers in the middle and the shorter ones on either end (see Chapter Four, Sections I and II, which deal with the formation of the choir) tentatively assigning bells so that the two octaves in the key of G are covered.

V. *Holding Bells*

Very briefly the director should demonstrate the various ways of holding the handbell. (See Chapter Three, Section I, which deals with general information on the various ways the fingers can grip the handbell.) Then he will have each ringer ring his bell or bells, beginning with either the highest or the lowest tone. After each ringer has had a turn, the director could have the choir ring the two diatonic octaves up or down the scale in a steady rhythm. The director should designate whether the ringer with the highest or lowest bell should start the ringing. He can then set the tempo by saying rhythmically, "one, two, three, four, five, six, ready, ring." The lowest or highest ringer begins on count "one" after the words "ready, ring." The ringing should begin without a break in tempo, and each ringer gets a turn as the director counts rhythmically up to fifteen. A slow tempo should be set at first. If there is a G 25 bell in the set it could be rung either before or after the two-octave scale line.

VI. *Free-Ring Period*

When each ringer has had a chance to ring individually, the director will want to initiate a free-ring period. This is a period of time for all ringers to practice rings simultaneously. This is a most important feature of all handbell choir sessions, and more especially the first few sessions as it gives them the feel of their particular handbells and a chance to perfect the straight as well as the more difficult rings. The director should have a signal, such as raising the hand, to indicate when the free-ring period is over. The purpose of this period, as well as the signal for stopping the free ringing, should be clearly indicated by the director. If at any time the director feels these few minutes are not worthily spent, he should stop the group and go on to the next part of the rehearsal.

The signal for the cessation of the free-ring period should be the most important directive for the new ringers to have firmly established in mind, and it should be used anytime a director wants undivided attention from his group. The use of this visual signal prevents the director from having to speak against a disorderly combination of bells and voices, and is especially valuable when several handbell choirs come together for a rehearsal or performance.

VII. *Scale Ringing and Ringing Changes*

Although it is difficult to have good scale ringing with a new handbell choir, the director will want to try some at the first rehearsal. He will either start at the bottom or the top of the scale (as indicated in the preceding section) having first a straight ring up and down, and then trying a front double or a back ring up and down.

There should be some of this scale ringing at each rehearsal, practicing various rings and ringing in thirds, fifths, sixths, or octaves. These intervals can also be rung as broken chords rather than together. When a choir works out scale ringing for performance this ringing is called "handbell changes" or simply "changes." This, however, is much different from the traditional change ringing practiced in England.*

---

* Traditional change ringing follows a mathematical pattern using available bells (especially tower bells) in a prescribed order. The first steps in change ringing are explained in *Elementary Change Ringing*, by F. F. Rigby, S.P.C.K., London, 1956.

Scale ringing either alone, or in combination with chordal progressions, is a good device to use for any necessary modulations when performing in a unit several short numbers which may be in a variety of keys.

VIII. *Simple Melodies*

The director should choose a simple tune or two which the ringers know and like, and have them play it as he points to each person when it is his turn to ring. If there is a member of the choir who would like to point out a tune, he should be encouraged. (See Chapter Six, Section III, which deals with melody line ringing.)

IX. *Introduction to the Chart*

Even if the choir does not have time during the first rehearsal to actually play from a chart, there should be one or two available for the choir to see. The director might have them read the first phrase of music from one of the charts, or perhaps just the melody of the first phrase, depending on the abilities of the ringers. (See Chapter Six, Section I, 1, A, which deals with the use of charts for beginners.) This would give the choir some idea of how a chart is used. However, no one part of the first session or two should be overworked to the point of tiring the ringers. The director should always be conscious of keeping the spirit of fun alive during rehearsals, and he should be especially mindful of this at the first rehearsal.

X. *Teaching without Bells*

It is possible to conduct rehearsals before the arrival of handbells. Any object (such as a pencil) can be used instead of a bell, and the potential ringers develop a feel for the arm and wrist movement essential for good ringing by pretending to ring these imaginary bells. Acquaintance with handbell music is made and each member of the group is assigned a note or notes just as ordinarily would be done. As each ringer pretends to ring his note he also sings the tone, thus developing an ability for sight-singing as well as becoming acquainted with the music he will later actually ring.

It is also possible to use the small Swiss-type* toy bells, or to use glasses filled with water, tuned to various pitches. However, the use of either of these objects, while lots of fun and helpful rhythmically, does not teach the proper wrist movement. Actually for developing all-around good musicianship, the singing of the pitches is more challenging and helpful, although initially it would certainly add interest to make some use of toy bells, water glasses or some similar objects.

The first rehearsal without actually ringing handbells should hold the same dramatic interest as the first session with the bells. However, to capture the potential ringer's imagination, even more careful preparation on the part of the director is necessary.

---

* A Swiss-type bell is one which must be rung by holding the mouth of the bell predominantly downward, as the clapper stem of this type bell is usually a linked chain rather than solid metal. The Melodè Bell is an accurately pitched toy bell which has been used successfully to aid in teaching music fundamentals to countless grade school pupils.

CHAPTER NINE

Codes and Awards

I. *Purpose of a Code*

Because being in an active bell choir is a special privilege, directors should expect extra faithfulness and work from the ringers. Many handbell choirs have a great *esprit de corps*, while other choirs, sometimes within the same church, will need detailed standards to guide the members.

A choir which has a second choir working on identical repertoire and which uses this second choir to provide substitute ringers for rehearsals and performances (see Chapter Five, Section V, 1, which deals with the subject of providing substitute ringers) will usually not need much in the code concerning faithful attendance. However, any system used for obtaining substitutes should be explained in the code.

II. *Preparation of a Code*

As rehearsals progress the director should keep in mind certain important areas, such as attendance, progress in memorization, and the general attitude of the ringers. If the director feels that higher standards should be maintained, it is usually good to have two or three volunteers, or ringers with outstanding records, to work with the director in making up a code for the choir.

Some choirs have officers. This is an especially good plan for boys' choirs, particularly of junior high age, because they often function better as a club. Through brief business meetings the boys have some say in the government of the group and in the planning of trips or other extra-curricular events. When choirs have officers, they can work with the director in formulating an adequate code or set of rules, or other members of the choir can be appointed or elected to work with the director.

III. *An Example of a Code*

The following code could not be used by all handbell choirs, as it would not specifically meet the needs of all ringing groups. It merely serves as an illustration and as a guide for the director who may be planning a code or standards for his own group. Actually the illustration given is one that was used for a two-day bell choir program that worked integrally with a singing program. As must be the case with any code, this example was actually used to meet a particular set of problems.

In order to execute a code which involves keeping a record of each bell ringer's progress, it is advisable to have an assistant present to take down and tabulate information during rehearsals.

Code of the Bell Ringers

Each bell ringer must have:

1. Good standing in the singing choir.
2. On a basis of two rehearsals per week, no more than one unexcused absence, plus no more than two excused absences in any two-month period, making a total of no more than three absences in any two-month period. Three latenesses equal one absence. Excused absences are those which the director knows about *before* the beginning of the rehearsal.
3. Music books ready for inspection at each rehearsal — notes played are to be circled or underlined, pages reinforced with circular tabs when inserted in notebooks, and the ini-

tial of each ringer's note or notes should appear at least one inch tall on the top right side of the cover. If the director finds a notebook not in order, the ringer receives a demerit.

4. Music completely memorized for the rehearsal which follows its issuance by seven days. The director may at any time during a rehearsal ask a bell ringer to play his part alone saying the words and numbers aloud or ringing with the piano. If he fails to play it correctly after the second attempt he receives a demerit. (If help is needed, the time to get it is after one of the weekday choir rehearsals.)

5. A good record in rehearsals; *i.e.*, no chattering, gum chewing, or asking questions without first raising a hand and being called upon by the director. If the director must call a person's name the second time in a single rehearsal to bring him to attention, that person automatically leaves the room and takes a demerit.

Further general rules:

6. A bell ringer can have no more than five demerits in any two-month period.

7. Although bells are permanently assigned with the ringer usually having these same bells, it may become necessary in some musical numbers for the director to distribute the parts differently, depending on the number of accidental tones used and the frequency with which they occur. The ringer must be prepared to ring any bell, and should enjoy the opportunity of becoming accustomed to a new bell or bells.

8. If a ringer fails to notify the director of his absence *before* a rehearsal, the director may assign *all* his parts to those ringers present.

9. At the discretion of the director, some bell ringers with only one note assigned may be called upon to memorize a second note, only to be played if and when the original assignee is sick.* This second assignment will be subject to the same rules as the original.

10. Ringers must assume complete responsibility for acquiring music issued at any rehearsal they have missed.

11. Bell ringers must expect extra duties from time to time; *e.g.*, directing, assembling music, taking attendance, etc.

12. Members of the bell choir are under the same rehearsal rules as listed under 5, regardless of whether or not the regular director is in charge or another member of the bell choir appointed by the director.

13. Being a member of the handbell choir does not necessarily guarantee the assignment of a note in each musical number, as occasionally, due to the nature of the music, this is impossible.

14. In the event that it becomes necessary, a second bell choir can be organized for new ringers and any experienced ringers who do not meet the standards enumerated but who want to continue working with handbells at a slower pace. Ringers in this second choir may participate in *all* social outings, but would not ring as frequently in performance.

IV. *Awards*

It is usually good for the church to present an award to the ringers at the end of a choir year. This award can either be

---

* Only an exceptionally fine ringer could be asked to memorize a single piece of music two ways; *i.e.*, with the one note, and when needed, ringing two notes. It is more advisable, when possible, to have regular substitutes or to have a two-choir system. (See Chapter Five, Section V, 1, which deals with the subject of substitutes.)

a personal one for the ringer to keep or, preferably, it can be an award which is worn on the robe the following year. This latter system provides more incentive for the ringers to remain loyal. The award can also take the form of a group award such as a trip.* A personal award should be given to the faithful ringer who must leave the choir, either because he is going away to school or moving with his family.

Awards can be given to ringers who meet minimal standards or they can be given only for outstanding merit. Perhaps a director will want to issue awards to all those who have satisfactorily participated in the program. He may want to give some special tribute or gift to the ringer who has done much more than was required in the regular program. If a ringer is to be singled out, his extra contribution to the overall program must be of such quality that there is no doubt in anyone's mind that he deserves special recognition. If a director uses some system of demerits, such as illustrated in the code in the previous section, the ringer or ringers receiving special recognition would have records largely free from demerits.

In order to determine which ringers deserve awards, when all ringers are not to receive them equally, some directors utilize a point system whereby for each job done well (*i.e.*, memorizing music, attendance, attention in rehearsal, etc.) a certain number of points is earned.

Another method for determining the ringer or ringers with the highest merit is to begin with 100%, and for each rehearsal missed or assignment unprepared take off 1%. A director can set a certain per cent essential for achieving an award or special recognition.

---

* Some churches supplement the money earned by the ringers for their trip, which may be to a festival or purely for entertainment.

Actually, because of the high demands placed on all ringers in a carefully set up and executed program, it would seem wise that all ringers successfully completing a year of service should receive an award.

CHAPTER TEN

Uses for Bells in Worship

I. *The Prelude*

Handbells played during the prelude to the service of worship are very effective. They can form the complete prelude, or can be used as a part of it, following or preceding organ music. Handbells used at this time can be played either alone, with soft organ accompaniment, or they can be used in a regular organ number arranged so that the bells have a prominent part. An effective number which can be used as a prelude is "Alla Trinita," arranged for organ and handbells.

If the handbells are going to be rung only at this time during the service, it is often advisable that the choir be at least partially visible to the congregation since the actual physical act of ringing provides some interest. The choir can stand on the chancel steps, around the back of an organ console which is centered in the chancel, or in any other suitable location in front of or out of sight of the congregation. When the organ is being used with the handbells it is good to have the ringers as near the organist as possible so that there can be greater team work. If, however, handbells are to be rung during the service, it would probably be better to have the ringers take their places in the balcony or the narthex of the church for the prelude, provided the choir is not ringing with organ accompaniment. The congregation, having heard the bells but not having seen them, would experience added pleasure in seeing them ring at a later point in the service.*

---

* The use of handbells in the prelude is discussed more fully in *A letter from The Handbell Choir Loft*, Vol. I, No. 2, November 1958, p. 9.

II. *Processionals and Recessionals*

When the handbell choir is used on the processional or recessional hymn it processes as a singing choir, ringing on one or two of the several stanzas of the hymn. The handbell choir can ring the introduction by playing the handbell arrangement all the way through, or on long processionals (especially at festivals) in addition to ringing the introduction they can ring a stanza as an interlude either alone or with the organ. In order to give the congregation and singing choirs additional support in singing the opening phrase of the hymn when the bells take the introduction, the organ can join the handbell choir in one of the concluding phrases of the introduction, beginning softly and building up the organ to a full bell and organ conclusion.

Only handbell arrangements which follow the harmonic structure of the hymn as written in the hymnal should be used for processionals or recessionals using bells, voices and organ simultaneously.

When the bells are ringing an introduction, the congregation should be prepared by having this fact noted in the bulletin; *i.e.*, "Introduction by handbell choir" or "Introduction by handbells and organ." Otherwise the congregation might not know when to begin singing.

III. *Descants*

Handbell descants are most effective when rung either with small congregations or on the more quiet hymns. However, at festival times when several choirs ring the descant together, it is especially effective as it has greater carrying power.

Another use of the descant is to ring it with the organ on the introduction of a hymn. All kinds of hymns lend themselves beautifully to the combination of bells and organ. The descant

91

can also be used on a stanza or two of the hymn. Even when the ringing is almost impossible to hear above the organ and congregational singing, it lends a certain fullness which contributes to the overall effectiveness of a hymn.

When a descant is rung with the organ on the introduction it is important to note this fact in the bulletin so that the people will be prepared to sing on the first stanza.

A handbell descant and a straight handbell arrangement (which do not conflict harmonically) can be used together when several choirs are participating in the same service.

IV. *Accompaniment for Hymn Singing*

Occasionally the director will want to have either an entire hymn or a stanza or two sung with only the accompaniment of handbells. This accompaniment can either be a regular full arrangement (see "All Hail the Power of Jesus' Name") or a descant written especially for unison or *a cappella* singing. This descant can be used alternately with the regular arrangement. (See the arrangement of the hymn tune *St. Catherine.*) When handbells are to be used solely as the accompaniment for hymn singing, they should also ring the introduction, and this fact should be noted in the bulletin.

V. *Responses*

There are various places in the service of worship where it is appropriate to incorporate handbell responses. These responses can be adapted from choral responses, amens, short hymn tunes, or from a phrase or two of a longer hymn. (See "Softly Now the Light of Day.") These responses can be used during the sacrament of infant baptism in place of a choral

response, after prayers, during the presentation of the offering*
or after the final benediction.

Some responses sound best alone, but often a soft organ
accompaniment adds color. Responses can be harmonic, using
a full bell arrangement, or they can be purely melodic. In rung
responses, pure melodic line is usually more effective with
organ than without. However, there are some instances in which
the utter simplicity of melodic line creates a mood which can
easily be destroyed by any embellishments from the organ.

When responses are rung the ringers should be as incon-
spicuous as possible, taking their places to the side or to the
rear of the church. Although the ringers should ring from a
position as nearly out of view of the congregation as possible,
their position must be favorable to the tone of the handbells.
When possible there should be a solid wall behind the choir to
reflect the tone and add resonance. Most choirs find it necessary
to experiment to determine the position in the church which
contributes the greatest resonance to the ringing.

VI. *Prayer Hymns*

Occasionally the minister may want to use the bell choir
to set a mood for prayer. This mood can be set either before or
after the words "Let us pray" are spoken.

Often when a handbell choir is visiting a church, it is
effective to have the first ringing in the service come during the

---

* Handbells can be used during the presentation of the offering by having the
bells repeat the sung response. For example, in churches where during the
presentation of the offering the *Doxology* is sung followed by a prayer of dedication, it is effective for special services to have the handbell choir repeat the
Doxology (either with or without soft organ accompaniment) after the congregation has sung it. The minister would have to be aware of this so he would
wait until the bells had concluded before giving the prayer of dedication. If
"Our Father's God to Thee" is sung after the prayer of dedication, the handbell
choir can repeat it. This provides music while the ushers return to the back of
the church.

prayer, after the minister says "Let us pray." Then there is complete quiet in the church, and as eyes are closed or averted from the ringers, the congregation is able to hear without distraction the sheer beauty of the music of the bells. As they listen, the worshippers are drawn closer to God.

As in the case of the handbell response, the prayer hymn should be performed with a minimum of attention drawn to the ringers. Also, it is best not to note this hymn in the bulletin, but rather to have it come as a surprise, with any necessary details worked out ahead of time with the minister.

VII. *Anthems*

Regular handbell arrangements or organ numbers with an added handbell score can be used in place of a sung anthem. As in the case of the prelude, the handbell arrangements can be rung with or without organ accompaniment. However, the more elaborate bell arrangements are complete in themselves and are usually most effective when rung alone.

Regular anthems arranged for bells and voices, or for bells, voices and organ are generally the best suited to this part of the service. (See "Vesper Hymn.") The singing can be done either by the singing choirs or by the ringers themselves. If the ringers do the singing it is usually best to have unison singing.* Occasionally a choir will be able to master two-part treble singing and ring simultaneously. If the vocal parts are regular S.A.T.B. music, they should be done by the singing choir, except in the very rare instance when the ringers are also expert singers and there is a balanced distribution of the parts.

* This should not be attempted unless it can be done well. As well as musicianship, the ability of ringers to attempt singing depends mainly on the composition of the group; *i.e.*, a mixed choir or one with changing voices should not attempt singing with ringing.

When the bell choir joins the regular singing choir or choirs in presenting an anthem in which bells and voices interweave, the ringers and singers should be placed together. This makes it easier for voices and bells to balance.

When the bell score is complicated and the handbell choir is performing with the singing choir, it is usually best to have a separate director for the bells. The bell choir director should be able to see the organist or choir director easily. The bell choir should rehearse with the singing choir at least once, and because there are usually more singers than ringers, the bell ringers should arrange to attend the regular singing choir rehearsal. Also, when bells are being used in the anthem, it is good to have a final rehearsal of all choirs just preceding the service of worship.

VIII. *Two-Choir Possibilities*

Antiphonal ringing can be done if the church has two sets of bells, or during handbell choir festivals when several choirs are present. A bell arrangement with identical phrases is often effective, having one choir ring a phrase and another echo it from a distance; or a complete number can be rung, having another choir echo it or ring a second more elaborate version.

Two or more choirs can also ring together. Choirs ringing together can lend more tone to an arrangement. The most impressive touch to a festival comes when many choirs ring together on a hymn, actually dominating the organ and the congregational singing.

IX. *An Example of a Festival Service:*
PRELUDE
 "Kyrie, God, Holy Spirit" .... *Bach*
 "Carillon" .... *Sowerby*
 "Trisagion on NICAEA" .... *Griffiths*

THE HANDBELL CHOIR

PROCESSIONAL HYMN

"All glory, laud and honor" .... ST. THEODULPH
arr. Watson
CONGREGATION, ORGAN AND COMBINED HANDBELL CHOIRS

CALL TO WORSHIP

PRAYER OF INVOCATION

THE LORD'S PRAYER

ANTHEM "The Message of Bells" .... *Watson*
WEST SIDE PRESBYTERIAN HANDBELL CHOIR

Bells for freedom; bells for strength;
Bells for peace; bells for faith!
God, in this hour touch our hearts;
Leave the noise of discordant strife behind us,
That we may perceive that which is right, good and noble.
Purge from our souls all injured pride.
Build within us strength of deed, that with steadfast mind and heart
We may face the future of this land.
Encircle our lives with the ringing truth
That God's law must be sought.
— *Doris Watson*

THE FESTIVAL OF THE HOLY TRINITY
God The Father

(The creator of the universe, who has a personal concern for each of us.)

SCRIPTURE READING: Psalm 8

"Let us with a gladsome mind" .... MONKLAND
arr. Watson
FIRST CHURCH BELL RINGERS OF STATEN ISLAND

"Alleluia" .... *Mozart*
YORK HANDBELL CHOIR *arr. Parry*

"O wondrous type, O vision fair" .... DEO GRACIAS
WEST SIDE PRESBYTERIAN HANDBELL CHOIR *arr. Watson*

"Come, ye thankful people, come" .... ST. GEORGE'S WINDSOR
arr. Voester
"A mighty Fortress is our God" .... EIN' FESTE BURG
VILLAGE CHURCH BELL RINGERS *arr. Jouard*

HYMN "O God, our Help in ages past" .... ST. ANNE

96

God The Son

(God as revealed perfectly in human life in Jesus Christ our Saviour.)

SCRIPTURE READING: John 1:1-5, 9-14, 16-18

"Jesus, Lover of my soul" .... ABERYSTWYTH
arr. Watson
WEST SIDE PRESBYTERIAN HANDBELL CHOIR
FIRST CHURCH BELL RINGERS OF STATEN ISLAND

"Beautiful Saviour" .... SCHÖNSTER HERR JESU
arr. Conover
CRESCENT AVENUE PRESBYTERIAN HANDBELL CHOIR

"Be Thou my Vision" .... SLANE
YORK HANDBELL CHOIR   *arr. Grover*

"Come, ye faithful, raise the strain" .... ST. KEVIN
arr. Grambling
MOUNTAIN LAKES COMMUNITY CHURCH BELL RINGERS

"Now the green blade riseth" .... French
arr. Lancaster
SECOND PRESBYTERIAN CHURCH HANDBELL CHOIR

HYMN   "O sons and daughters" .... O FILII ET FILIAE
INTRODUCTION BY HANDBELLS   *arr. Watson*
(The congregation will rise and sing the entire hymn except
the fourth stanza which the handbells will ring alone.)

THE OFFERING

ANTHEM   "Vesper Hymn" .... VESPER HYMN
arr. Watson
WEST SIDE PRESBYTERIAN HANDBELL CHOIR

Hark! the vesper bells are ringing,
Bringing beauty to this hour.
In the fullness of this worship,
May we know God's calming power.

Teach us, with Thy love unfailing
In this hour Thy truth to see;
That with hearts and voices singing
We will strive to follow Thee.

Jubilate, Jubilate, Jubilate! Amen.   *— Doris Watson*

DOXOLOGY

PRAYER OF DEDICATION

God The Holy Spirit

(The divine spark within every man which can respond to the resurrected Christ who is with us still.)

SCRIPTURE READING: Acts 2:1-8, 12-13, 38-39

"Alla Trinita" .... *XIV Century Melody*
arr. Dickinson-Watson
WEST SIDE PRESBYTERIAN HANDBELL CHOIR

"Onward, Christian soldiers" .... ST. GERTRUDE
VILLAGE CHURCH BELL RINGERS *arr. Eckel-Voester*

"Come, labor on" .... ORA LABORA
YORK HANDBELL CHOIR *arr. Grover*

"Once to every man and nation" .... TON-Y-BOTEL
arr. Grambling
MOUNTAIN LAKES COMMUNITY CHURCH BELL RINGERS

"Christ of the upward way" .... SURSUM CORDA
arr. Lancaster
SECOND PRESBYTERIAN CHURCH HANDBELL CHOIR

"Jacob's Ladder" .... *Spiritual*
WEST SIDE PRESBYTERIAN HANDBELL CHOIR *arr. Watson*
FIRST CHURCH BELL RINGERS OF STATEN ISLAND

HYMN "Faith of our fathers" .... ST. CATHERINE
descant by Watson
CONGREGATION, ORGAN AND COMBINED HANDBELL CHOIRS

VESPER PRAYER

BENEDICTION

CHORAL RESPONSE .... *Spanish*
Let us now depart in Thy peace, Blessed Jesus;
Send us to our homes with God's love in our hearts.
Let not the busy world claim all our loyalties.
Keep us ever mindful, dear Lord, of Thee. Amen. *Anon.*

HANDBELL AMEN

RECESSIONAL HYMN

"All hail the power of Jesus' Name!" .... CORONATION
arr. Watson
CONGREGATION, ORGAN AND COMBINED HANDBELL CHOIRS

SILENT MEDITATION (The congregation seated)

POSTLUDE

"Carillon" .... *Vierne*
(A list of the participating handbell choirs and clergy should appear at the end of the program.)

CHAPTER ELEVEN

Program Planning

I. *Planning for a Purpose*

Despite the fact that the choir will make some attempt to limit engagements other than ringing for services of worship (see Chapter One, Section I, which deals with the role of the handbell choir) there will be many times when it will seem right to accept a program engagement.

In planning the program the director will want to keep in mind the occasion, the approximate age of the audience and any past experience they may have had with music or handbell ringing, and the amount of time to be consumed by the ringing program. The type of occasion will determine the degree of formality or informality of the presentation. Sometimes a program chairman will want a group of three or four numbers presented in the framework of a larger program. Provided there is an overall master of ceremonies for the program, and the timing of the music is to be fairly accurate, the director's responsibility will be primarily to select and time the music. If the director is asked to provide an entire program of a half hour to an hour in length, in almost all situations the music should be presented in an informal verbal framework; and to some extent, there should be audience participation.

To determine what emphasis should be developed in the program, the director should find out from the program chairman the purpose he has in asking the handbell choir to ring. This can range from sheer listening enjoyment to providing an

31320

incentive to a group for having its own choir. The director should also talk over with the program chairman his idea of keeping a handbell presentation informal, to see if there is any decided reaction one way or another to this suggestion. In a few circumstances it is not possible, or advisable, to have audience participation, and if this is the case, the director should know it before attempting to plan the program.

II. *Specific Suggestions*

The following are some ideas to keep in mind when planning a program:

1. *Select the music:* Pick out the numbers which the ringers know best; and if there is ample time for preparation, select additional music which may best illustrate any point you may want to cover in your spoken presentation.

2. *Organize the program:* Think of the ideas you want to cover and arrange them in what seems to be a good order. Then fit the music as appropriately as possible around the spoken framework.

3. *Remember the audience:* Consider ways to get audience participation:

A. Through the demonstration of special rings: Have a ringer demonstrate the ring and teach a volunteer from the audience.

B. By ringing in a special number: Have a volunteer come up forward and ring in a number which is done in single note or octave ringing. (See Chapter Six, Section III, which deals with melody line ringing.) The director should choose a bell which rings fairly frequently. Before the volunteer attempts to ring in the number, the ringer who ordinarily plays the bell should demonstrate the technique involved in straight ringing, letting the volunteer try the ring until he does it fairly accurately.

C. Have the audience sing with the bells: (This is often a good way to conclude a program or to provide a break in a lengthy program. It should be a very familiar song, arranged simply and in a good key for group singing.) Have the audience stand and have the ringers play the number all the way through for an introduction, and then have the audience sing with the ringing. Usually it is best to have the singing done on just the first stanza, so there is no problem with words.

4. *Get acquainted*: Toward the beginning of the program be sure to include some time for the audience to get to know the ringers individually. An easy way to do this is to start from the bottom or top of the choir and have each ringer announce his name (and perhaps age or grade in school when ringing for young audiences) and then ring the bell or bells he plays, giving the name of the note.

5. *Interest the audience*: Keep the element of surprise alive in a program. Don't always tell an audience the name of a number before ringing it. See if someone can identify it. It is especially good when working with young audiences to keep their interest by having them listen for something. Perhaps after explaining a certain ring you might have the audience try to hear it in an actual piece of music. Or if a choir rings the *Cambridge Quarters*, it might be interesting to tell the audience the time of Sunday morning worship through the striking of the hour bell.

6. *Watch the clock*: Never agree to provide a program of more than an hour. A program of thirty to forty-five minutes

is more desirable. Ringing is not a variety show, and a high point of interest should be maintained throughout the presentation period.

7. *Interest the choir*: If possible, present some new idea, joke or new music on each program so the ringers themselves will be more interested and challenged. A happy choir conveys the Christian Gospel much more rapidly than an obviously bored choir. For example, if the choir is capable, have them ring a new single note number as the director points it out. This makes the ringers alert and pleases them when they do well. On the other hand, never do anything surprising that is beyond the choir's ability.

8. *Use a chart*: You may want to bring a chart and demonstrate its use. In a workshop situation the members of the group can try ringing from the charts.

9. *Follow through*: Scrap books or charts illustrating handbell ringing or containing bits of publicity can be made available to an audience at the close of the program.

SUMMATION

The most exciting element in working with handbells is the opportunity for creative thinking. The methods described in this manual have come about through trial and error. Other methods are possible, but those outlined in this manual have worked for the author, and it is hoped they will be helpful to others. However, in working with a handbell choir it is important to look for new vistas, to keep the spirit of creativity alive.

The church that has a handbell program finds that both its worship and fellowship life are strengthened. The very nature of handbell ringing demands an integral relationship of the ringers with each other. It is believed that any church, school or community group can be enriched by inaugurating a full handbell program.